ON ILKLA MOOAR BAHT 'AT

Dedication

To Stanley Evans, with whom I first walked over Ilkley Moor, and Ian Dewhirst, with whom I share the pleasures of dialect and local history.

On Ilkla Mooar baht 'at

The Story of the Song

Arnold Kellett

First published in 1998 by
Smith Settle Ltd
Ilkley Road
Otley
West Yorkshire
LS21 3JP

ISBN Paperback 1 85825 108 7
Hardback 1 85825 109 5

British Library Cataloguing-in-Publication data:
A catalogue record for this book is available from the British Library.

Set in Plantin.

Designed, printed and bound by
SMITH SETTLE
Ilkley Road, Otley, West Yorkshire LS21 3JP

Contents

Acknowledgements

I would like to record my gratitude to Richard Whiteley of Yorkshire Television for kindly providing a foreword, to Peter Kearney for the cover and map, to Wallace Harvey for useful information, to Kingsley Empett for generously loaning illustrations, to Stanley Evans and Dr Ian Dewhirst for comments and illustrations, and especially to Pat (my Mary Jane) for her customary invaluable support.

In addition to those mentioned in the text my thanks are also due to the following helpful people and organisations:

Derek Arnold (White Wells), Philip Bambridge (centenary photo), Linda Baxter, Beatrice Benge, Arthur Blackhurst, Betty Carman (Cranbrook Museum), David Cousins (Heritage Services, Canterbury), Bob Duckett (Bradford Reference Library), P G Elgey, English Folk Dance and Song Society, Brendan Flynn, Vic Gale (Dick Hudson's), Halifax Reference Library, David Hanson (*Halifax Courier*), Harrogate Reference Library, Janet Henderson, (Methodist Church Music Society), Huddersfield Reference Library, Andrew Johnson, Denis Kilcommons (*Huddersfield Examiner*), Peter Lazenby (*Yorkshire Evening Post*), Leach Lithoprint Ltd (Brighouse), Leeds Reference Library, Ralph Moore, Dr Pat Morris, Marie Cure Cancer Care, Kathleen Pinder (Ilkley Tourist Information Centre), Barrie Rhodes, Geoff Riley, Julia Smith, Margaret Smith, Arthur D Walker, Rev Michael Walling (Canterbury), Arnold Watson, Carl Willetts, Paul Wilson (National Sound Archive).

Colour photographs are by the author unless otherwise stated.

Foreword

I have lived within five miles of Ilkley Moor all my life. I have driven past the Cow and Calf countless times. I have marvelled at the view of Ilkley, and the Wharfe Valley beyond, on every single occasion. I pass the topmost point and begin the steep descent down Cowpasture Road. And yet — how many times have I stopped? How many times have I trekked round the Cow and Calf or ambled over to White Wells?

Very few, I'm afraid. Just as Londoners rarely go to the Tower of London or watch the changing of the Guard. They are proud enough of the fine tradition they represent, but with all the arrogance of familiarity they give it a miss. So it is with me and Ilkley Moor. Give me a chance to talk about it when I am two hundred miles away — well, I'm so proud of it and so knowledgeable, you would think I owned it.

I have been known to wax lyrical about the moor, the song, the town — the whole distillation of all that is best in Yorkshireness which Ilkley represents — and people have gasped open-mouthed at my easy knowledge and possessive pride about the place. But I have to admit, even though I look out every day on the environs of the moor and even though bewildered moorland sheep sometimes inquire at my gate, I know very little.

Which is why I welcome Arnold Kellett's work. In the following pages there lies the truth about Ilkley and *On Ilkla Mooar baht 'at*. If, like me, you have tended to over-exaggerate your personal connection with Ilkley, this noble work will not only give you essential information, it will be an invaluable tool for every Yorkshire person to extol the virtues of Ilkley and its song with conviction, passion and sincerity.

Well done, Arnold! And thanks.

Richard Whiteley
Yorkshire Television

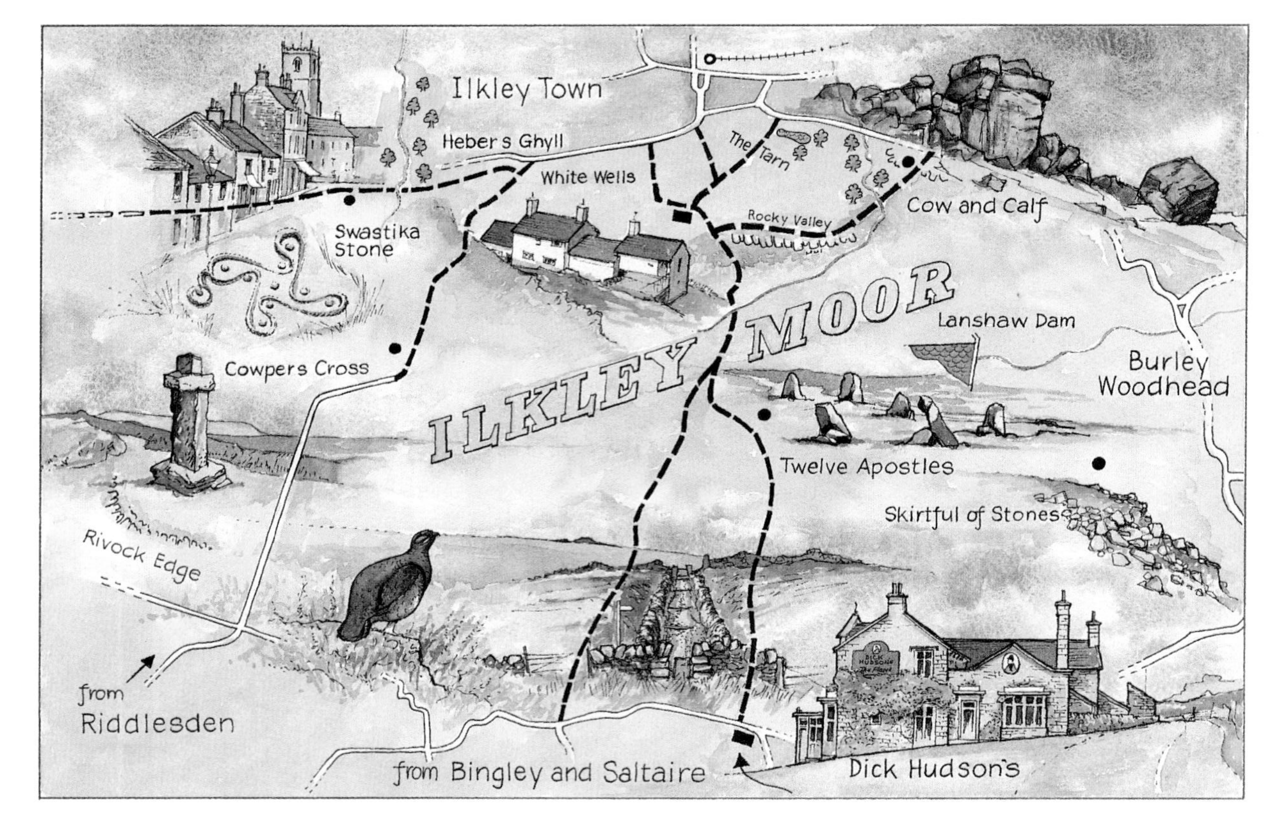

Sketch map of Ilkley Moor, with well-known locations superimposed (not to scale).

The Magic of Ilkley Moor

In writing this book I feel I can take nothing for granted. So much mystery, confusion and downright ignorance surrounds this song ... a television presenter recently remarked that he thought it had been written by people from Derbyshire ... an otherwise excellent guide-map published by the Ramblers' Association declares it to have been composed 'by a Lincolnshire clergyman' ... an American book of folk songs introduces it as 'an old Welsh folk song' ... and one of the commonest questions asked at the Ilkley Tourist

The Cow and Calf Rocks, the most popular meeting place on Ilkley Moor. Ever since Victorian times, people have come here to sing the song, especially Yorkshire exiles from overseas.

Information Centre — by English visitors as well as foreigners — is this: 'Please can you tell me where *Baht 'at* is?'

My purpose, then, is to set the record straight, and to present the world-famous song *On Ilkla Mooar baht 'at* in the fullest possible context, paying due attention to the historical background from which it emerged. This does not mean that I shall be able to give clear-cut answers concerning its origin. As we tread the borderland between fact and fancy, much will remain elusive — and yet that is what makes the investigation worthwhile.

At first sight the song might seem no more than a curiosity — a bit of fun in quaint dialect, scarcely worthy of academic attention. All is not what it seems, however, and I can only say that probing beneath the surface has led me into discoveries and observations of unsuspected interest, which I would now like to share with the reader.

So, to begin at the beginning, let us have a look at the location whose name has been taken round the world by the title of the song. Of course, even without this kind of publicity, Ilkley Moor would have been well known in its own right. It was, after all, its existing popularity as a place for outings and rambles that brought the song into being.

A Land of Legend

From ancient times, mountains, hills and remote moors have always held a fascination for people living in the valleys below. This is certainly true of Ilkley Moor, rising to 1,323 feet (403m), which not only had its high places of magic and religion, but was where successive prehistoric peoples lived. A glance at one of the maps in the first volume of the *Victoria County History* shows the moor prominently marked as 'Neolithic implements in abundance' — just one indication of the amount of archaeological interest that the moor has offered over the years, especially in Victorian times. Along with the scientific approach of archaeologists and historians went a romantic interest in legend and folklore, kept alive by the very names of features on the moor — the Cow and Calf Rocks, the Pancake Rock, the Idol Rock, the Ashlar Chair, the Skirtful of Stones, Cowpers Cross, the Twelve Apostles and other stone circles, the Swastika Stone and the many boulders marked with the cryptic cup and ring symbol.

Harry Speight, one of the last of the Victorian writers to comment on Ilkley Moor, defines it in the memorable words:

> that wide and noble expanse of rugged moorland which rises above Ilkley, with its life-giving breezes, pleasant walks and memories of primeval occupation ...

How far back does that occupation go? Perhaps even to the dawn of humanity, when the area was under the awesome rule of a giant called Rombald. Ilkley Moor, covering some 1,700 acres (610ha), a roughly oval mass of high ground separating Airedale to the south from Wharfedale to the north, is part of the much larger Rombalds Moor. Though popularly said to have been named after the mythical Giant Rombald, nobody knows where this name came from. Speight gives the various forms in which it has turned up in documents — Rumbles, Rummell, Romall, Rumbald, Rombald — and thinks it may be derived either from the name of an obscure saint, Rumold, who lived around AD 775, or from the first Norman overlords, the family of de Romille. To this family belonged 'young Romilly', who was drowned in the Strid when a greyhound on a leash held back as he jumped — a tragedy commemorated in a poem by Wordsworth.

Whatever the origin of the name Rombald, or the notion that he was a giant, he is featured briefly, though dramatically, in local legend. The Cow and Calf Rocks owe their separate existence, it is said, to the mighty Rombald, who once took a gigantic stride across Wharfedale from Almscliff Crag, seven miles (11km) away. He slipped and fell awkwardly, breaking the Calf rock from the side of the Cow. Rombald's huge footprint can still be seen, it is claimed, in the side of the Cow. Then there is the legend that when this happened, Rombald's wife, who was gats.ring boulders in her apron,

Ilkley Tarn and, beyond it, a glimpse of White Wells in its commanding position overlooking Wharfedale.

dropped them towards the eastern end of the moor — where you can still see what is known as the Skirtful of Stones. A similar story is told about her having dropped the biggest boulder in Yorkshire, the Hitching Stone near Cowling.

When you have wandered over the moor, particularly when it is gloomy and misty, it is easy to see how strangely-shaped rocks of sombre millstone grit have given rise to legends and a feeling that the whole area is enveloped in mystery. Some of these rocks still baffle the experts. The strange cup and ring markings occur in this part of Yorkshire but nowhere else in England, some 200 of them in the area north of Bradford. The significance of the small circular depression in the rock, surrounded by a ring, has never been satisfactorily explained. Carved in the Early Bronze Age (about 1800 BC), they have variously been described as the indicators of nearby burials, representations of a prehistoric hut to entice spirits

Common flowers and plants of Ilkley Moor. Clockwise from top left: bracken, heather, moor mat grass, crowberry, bilberry, cross-leaved heath, cotton grass. (Stanley Evans)

away from the home of people who have died, representations of some object in the sky, including constellations, or something as simple as a territorial marking or a charm to ward off evil.

Even more mysterious is the elaborate carving in a rock above Woodhouse Crag on the north-western edge of the moor near Hebers Ghyll. This is the famous Swastika Stone, probably from later in the Bronze Age or the Early Iron Age. Named from a Sanskrit word for 'good fortune', this ancient symbol has been found in varying styles all over the world. Suggestions as to what it represents include the four winds and lightning, but more especially fire and the sun, both venerated by ancient peoples.

Visitors to Ilkley Moor have been inspired by these mysterious rocks to imagine the people associated with them, from the early

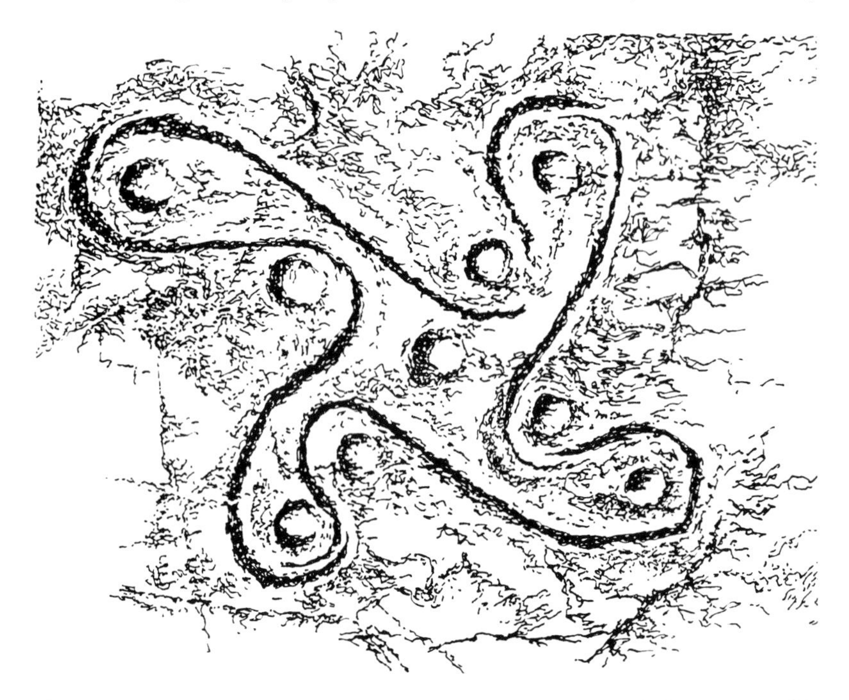

The Swastika Stone, which along with the ancient cup and ring stones adds magic and mystery to Ilkley Moor.

prehistoric ages to the coming of the Celts in about 500 BC. One visitor, Nicholas Size, a businessman who apparently came here for health reasons, wrote a short account of how the moor had affected him, published in 1934 as *The Haunted Moor*. In this he described a series of supernatural hallucinations he had experienced when walking over the remotest parts of the moor by himself. One area, not far from the Ashlar Chair, he named the 'Place of Horror', because when he came to it 'the air was full of groans and sobbing sounds, and all about there seemed to be corpses of injured people'. On another occasion, towards the end of the day, he saw a strange kind of fire on the top of the Cow Rock, with cloaked figures moving about near it. Then he saw that the face of the rock was glowing with 'some sort of phosphorescence'. He wondered if somebody had simply been lighting a fire, but when he examined the area the next morning could find no trace of one.

Nicholas Size seemed to be obsessed with the idea of human sacrifice on the moor. He imagined a priest standing by the Swastika Stone on which he would kill the victim, collecting the blood in two saucers carved into the rock. He later imagined he heard the screams of children being burnt alive in wicker cages by the Druids. He claimed he had a vision of a weird procession, accompanied by the sound of wailing voices:

> it all seemed to be coming from a long wraith of black mist which crept along the ancient green track ... from the direction of Keighley Gate past the Ashlar Stone, and was even now crossing the Dick Hudson track ... The figures were no more than shadows of unkempt-looking soldiers, armed with spears, axes and pall-staves, ... walking along there were women, with long streaming hair, all hurrying forward ... a score or so figures clad in white ... from all of them a continuance of the low wailing chant.

Whether this is taken at face value as an account of psychic experiences, or disregarded as neurotic fantasy, those who have walked the moor alone can well understand some people imagining it to be haunted by the ghosts of former pagan inhabitants.

All this seems a far cry from the cheerful band of singers who wandered this way singing their comic dialect song. But rambles over the moor are by no means always in bright sunshine, and when you consider the subject-matter of the song — death and burial on the moor — it is not perhaps all that different in the way it allows the moor to suggest such a morbid subject.

The Village of Ilkley

Following the little-understood prehistoric peoples came the Romans, building a fort overlooking the Wharfe, close to where the parish church now stands. To this they gave the name Olicana, the original Ilkley. Thought to have been founded in about AD 79 at the time of Agricola, it seems to have been burnt down by the Brigantes, then rebuilt in AD 197 by Virius Lupus. Little remains of it except the fragment of a wall and a grassy mound, but an extensive hypocaust under the commandant's house was uncovered in 1921, and the Manor House Museum contains many interesting remains and artefacts.

The later settlement of the Angles is well-attested in Ilkley by the remains of three early Christian crosses, formerly outside, but now restored and displayed inside the Parish Church of All Saints. The *Domesday Book* of 1086 records Ilkley as having a church with a priest, with half the manor wooded and the other half uncultivated. In 1252 Peter de Percy was granted the right to hold a fair each October and a market on Wednesdays. A little village with a market is what Ilkley remained for the next four centuries, and the moor above it was rarely visited except by those who wanted a shorter route into Airedale. All that was to change — as in the case of so many other once-insignificant places — with the discovery of a spring.

'The Mountain Spa'

Ilkley — and also its moor — owes its status to the fashion for taking the waters. The first place to be named a 'spa', after the town of that name in the Belgian Ardennes, was the Tewit Well, discovered in 1571 on what is now Harrogate Stray. Many centuries before this the town of Bath was visited for the healing waters of its hot saline springs, and the Romans built their famous baths there in about AD 76. It has been suggested that it was the Romans who first discovered Ilkley's potential as a spa, but there is no evidence to support this.

Unlike Harrogate, which had both the chalybeate water of the Tewit Well and the sulphur water of the Stinking Spaw, as well as many other mineral springs, the Ilkley water was simply a spring of clear, cold water flowing from the moor. It was discovered — or at least exploited — in about 1763 by Squire William Middleton at the place which soon came to be known as White Wells. The squire had two small stone baths built (one of which is still open to the public) and later a small charity bath for the poor, his intention being, not to provide water for drinking, as in many spas, but for the 'cold water cure'.

The idea was — and still is — that the health-seeker plunged into the icy-cold water and stayed there as long as possible. The vigorous rubbing with towels which followed was guaranteed to provide a warm glow and sense of renewed health. This kind of hydrotherapy had been pioneered in Malvern, which also possessed water without any particular mineral content. Soon Ilkley was being called the 'Malvern of the North', and well-to-do invalids and hypochondriacs started to visit the White Wells, now run by William Butler and his wife. They were taken in their carriages as far up the moor as possible, then walked the rest of the way, or rode on donkeys expert in negotiating the steep paths, in late Victorian times organised by the character affectionately known as 'Donkey Jackson'.

In 1841 the great connoisseur of spas, Dr A B Granville, described his visit to White Wells when he stayed in 'the village of Ilkley' with its moderately-priced boarding houses:

> The healing waters burst from the rocky mountain-side in a round, thick stream, at the rate repeatedly measured by myself,

of sixty gallons a minute. The temperature, 47°F, was only eight degrees lower than that of the surrounding atmosphere.

He gives a list of diseases the Ilkley water is said to have cured or relieved — scrofula, chronic inflamation of the eye, skin diseases, rheumatism, arthritis, stomach complaints and 'chronic weakness of the general system'. He quotes with approval from the account given by a medical colleague, Dr Adam Hunter, in 1819:

> The shock, on plunging into the Ilkley bath is excessive, and an irresistible impulse to escape from its influence is the first sensation produced. When this is accomplished, and the bather begins to dress, reaction almost immediately takes place, which is soon followed by a pleasant glow and lightness throughout the whole system. The body feels as relieved from a previous load, and unwonted energy and activity are communicated to the muscles of voluntary motion, while the mental sensations equally participate in the general animation.

Thus, in amusingly pompous style, we are given the reason for the crowds now coming to Ilkley — the invigoration produced by a cold bath. Dr Hunter recommends this treatment even for weak and infirm persons, in their case on alternate days, rather than the normal daily plunge. It is interesting to note that this praise of the water is coupled with one of the earliest mentions of Ilkley Moor itself as having health-giving properties:

> In this respect it excells any water with which I am acquainted. But a share of this quickening power must, in justice, be attributed to the bracing qualities of the mountain-breeze, which sweeps along in such ethereal purity.

Unlike most spas, which were situated in a shallow valley or on a plain, the White Wells were high up on the edge of the moor, commanding fine views of Wharfedale. For this reason Dr Granville rightly describes Ilkley as 'the Mountain Spa'.

Victorian Ilkley

Though visitors flocked to take the cold-water cure, providing a seasonal increase in residents, it was a long time before the population of Ilkley increased significantly, as these figures show:

1801	426 inhabitants
1851	811 "
1861	1,043 "
1891	5,767 "

In the early part of the Victorian period the town was essentially a base for visitors seeking health, not only at the spa, but in the surrounding countryside, which included such beauty-spots as Bolton Abbey. A guide published in 1829 shows that a third of the total number of dwellings were for visitors — three inns and thirty-six boarding-houses. Some of these visitors were of particular interest. Charlotte Brontë, for example, very much enjoyed her stay here in 1853, and we might imagine she would think of Ilkley Moor no less than the Haworth area, when she wrote:

Speak of the North — a lonely moor, silent and still and trackless lies ...

In the second half of the nineteenth century the village developed into a small town, now seen as an ideal place of residence for people who could afford to commute from the industrial cities to the south. A great boost to development was the opening of the first railway link with Ilkley on the 1st August 1865. The spa also continued to grow in Victorian times, with the building of substantial hydropathic establishments such as Craiglands, Troutbeck, Rockwood House, Wells House — and, most imposing of all, palatial Ben Rhydding, built in 1844 by a former mayor of Leeds at the enormous cost for those days of £30,000, originally housing eighty patients.

Ilkley's identity as a place synonymous with the recovery of health was celebrated by the 'Airedale Poet', John Nicholson, who is quoted in one of the Victorian guides published by Waddington's:

Victorian Ilkley in an early photograph of about 1870, looking down Church Street. (David Carpenter, *Ilkley The Victorian Era*)

> Ilkley, thy healthy mountains, wells and air
> Can cure the nervous, trembling in despair! ...
> To thee how many with their crutches come,
> Soon dance without them, and run smiling home ...
> Peace, Love and Solitude near Ilkley dwell,
> And health sits smiling at her mountain well.

However, the vast majority of Victorian visitors to Ilkley were not well-to-do hydrotherapy patients. They were ordinary working folk, drawn from the great populations of the nearby industrial towns. In 1892 Edmung Bogg, writing his *A Thousand Miles in Wharfedale*, broke into verse at the beauty of the heather, the song of the lark and curlew, and all the joys of the moorland — not for the wealthy, but for the workers, whom he imagined saying:

> Then away! Let us haste from the smoke-begirt towns,
> From the round of the dull and monotonous hours ...

Ilkley, for working people from the mill towns, was not only a spa, but a centre from which to enjoy the unspoilt countryside which stood in such contrast to Victorian urban life. This is the context in which *On Ilkla Mooar baht 'at* had its origin.

Walking on Ilkley Moor

Those staying in Ilkley — a 'gem set in heather', as *Bishop's Guide* called it — could take excursions to various parts of Wharfedale or travel as far afield as Harrogate, Knaresborough, Ripon and York. For the day-trippers we are concerned with, however, the town was essentially connected with walking on Ilkley Moor. The early guidebooks made the most of this, with enticing passages like the following:

> The Moor is a never-ending source of pleasure for all to whom a vast expanse of heather, rock-strewn, wild, yet beautiful, has any delight. Walking becomes a real pleasure, and the air acts like a tonic.

The routes followed in Victorian and Edwardian times are still there, and just as enjoyable. Several can be taken from the town itself, including the climb through wooded Hebers Ghyll to the Swastika Stone, and there is a choice of paths radiating from points such as the White Wells and the Cow and Calf. You can also walk on the moors above Burley Woodhead, where at one time it was possible to visit the 'Hermit of Rombalds Moor', the scruffy eccentric Job Senior, who lived in a hovel above the hamlet and was famous for his ability to sing bass, alto, tenor and soprano (though not all at the same time!). Lord Healey's favourite walk, when he lived in Riddlesden, was over the moor to Ilkley via Rivock Edge, also the route enjoyed by G K Chesterton, when he walked with his friend Father O'Connor, the original of 'Father Brown'.

The best-known of all the walks is undoubtedly the one from Dick Hudson's over the centre of the moor to Ilkley. As this is the one most likely to have been used by the first singers of the song, it is worth describing — and, better still, worth walking. The distance across to Ilkley is nearly four miles (6.5km), taking a leisurely couple of hours.

The start is just opposite the pub, up a stony track between walls. To the left you will see Eldwick Crag, and behind you increasingly fine views of Airedale. Soon you will reach rough grassland, then invasive bracken. If you are lucky you may see, as we did on recently walking this route, horses from the nearby stables galloping freely over this area. You enter the moor itself through a stile, following at first a paved pathway, later to become boggy in parts, but mostly dry and springy with the peat beneath. In August and September there is the purple ling all round you, and an occasional patch of pink cross-leaved heath. There would have been even more varieties of wild flowers and birds in Victorian times; as many as seventy different species of birds were once recorded in the area, including game birds. A little over halfway across the moor you will see just to the right of the path an ancient stone circle known as the Twelve Apostles, consisting of twelve irregular stones — Ilkley Moor's own miniature Stonehenge. The central part of the moor is fairly level, and when you reach the cairn and add your stone, it begins to descend.

After crossing the stream at the top of the ghyll you can take a narrower path, immediately to the right, which goes down towards the Cow and Calf. But the route that most Victorian walkers would have taken lies straight ahead. Soon you come to a broader path. The left-hand route is for White Wells. The right-hand route takes you first to the panoramic views from the top of Ilkley Crags, with

Rocky Valley below, then by a rough descent over the stream at the lower end of the ghyll, and on to the Cow and Calf Rocks.

Ilkley Today

Modern Ilkley is a pleasant town with an attractively compact centre, well known for its shops, especially in the Grove, where Betty's Café is situated. It is especially visited for its Literature Festival, founded in 1973. The moorland beauty spots known to Victorian visitors have changed remarkably little. White Wells, closed and neglected for many years, was rescued from dereliction by Eric Busby of Bradford in 1974 and is now open to the public for refreshments and a visit to the cold-plunge bath — still in operation, especially on occasions such as Yorkshire Day (for charity) and New Year's Day (when there is no charge).

A modern twist to the story of Ilkley Moor, which would have intrigued the more romantic of the Victorian visitors, is that it is known throughout the world as a place where there have been sightings of Unidentified Flying Objects and related phenomena. Nigel Mortimer, who takes parties of sky-watchers round the moor, claims that every year he receives 'two or three reports of close encounters with UFOs'. These include the report of the alien abduction of three Leeds ramblers who fell asleep near the Swastika Stone in 1983 and of a policeman in 1987 who was allegedly taken on board a UFO.

The busiest moorland area is the one around the Cow and Calf Rocks. These are impressive in themselves — the Cow, eighty feet by thirty-six feet and fifty feet high (24m x 11m x 15m), having been described as 'the largest detached block of stone in England'. A third rock, the Bull, even bigger, the size of a house, is said to have once stood here, but this seems to be a myth.

It is not often you can visit the Cow and Calf without seeing rock-climbers. But ordinary non-roped climbers can venture to the top of the Calf — footholes provided — and to the flatter top of the Cow, to enjoy the magnificent views. When I invited Sir Jimmy Savile to comment on the moors, he wrote:

> Ilkley is a magic name and a magic place. My world would have been so much less without the magic of the moors. Wherever I am in the world, a quick close of the eyes, and I am once again standing on top of the rocks, and everything is OK.

Cut into the rocks all round here, and especially on top of the Cow, you can see graffiti — the majority carved by Victorians. I have searched in vain for any reference to Mary Jane, but I feel sure that the first singers of *On Ilkla Mooar baht 'at* have left their mark here somewhere.

The Music of the Methodists

It comes as a surprise — even a shock — when you learn that the music of *On Ilkla Mooar baht 'at* is an old Methodist hymn tune. The second surprise — even the occasion of immediate disbelief — is when you further learn that the tune was written, not by a Yorkshireman, but by a Kentishman, a Canterbury boot and shoe-maker turned composer.

To explain the phenomenal success of this melody, I think we need to understand that its roots go deep into the evangelical revival of the eighteenth century and the work of John Wesley. So before we look at the circumstances in which it was written, it will be useful to fill in the background to the best-known hymn-singers in history — the people bearing the curious name of 'Methodist'.

John Wesley — a Brand from the Burning

Methodism was above all else a religious movement which emphasised genuine warmth of feeling, and in the beginning it was quite literally sparked off by a fire — the blazing home of the Rector of Epworth. In this old thatched rectory lived the Rev Samuel Wesley, his wife Susannah and their eight children. In the middle of the night of the 9th February 1709 fire broke out and, fanned by a north-east gale, it soon turned the house into a deadly inferno. All was confusion — the parents and their servants rushing around in their night-clothes, rousing the sleeping children. They managed to get them out into the garden, and were counting their heads, when they realised that one was missing — little Jacky (as John Wesley was then known), five and a half, still up there in his bedroom.

His father made three attempts to get back into the house, but the staircase was now ablaze and he was forced back by the fury of the flames. Then they saw a little face appear at the bedroom window. Jacky had climbed on a chest, and was trying to get out. The thatched roof above him was already on fire. What could they do? There was no ladder handy and it was too high for him to jump ... Suddenly, one of the neighbours had the presence of mind to put himself against the wall and get another, lighter, man to stand on his shoulders. The second man reached up and pulled the little boy out in the nick of time. At that very moment the blazing roof collapsed — fortunately falling inwards.

But for that dramatic rescue there would have been no John Wesley and no Methodism. In later life he constantly looked back to what he regarded as a stroke of providence, quoting from the book of Amos that he was 'a brand plucked from the burning'. After schooling at Charterhouse he went to Lincoln College, Oxford, where he became a lecturer as well as an ordained minister of the Church of England. While he was there his younger brother Charles came to the college as a student. At the time of the Epworth fire he had been a babe in arms. Now he was a keen young Christian, soon to become 'the sweet singer of Methodism', the world's most famous hymn-writer.

The Methodist Revival

It was Charles, not John, as is usually assumed, who started the little society of Oxford students who were determined to put their Church principles into practice. They not only met for regular prayer, Bible study and to take communion, but helped younger students, visited prisons and workhouses and taught the children of poor families. As the elder brother, John soon took over the leadership. The students started making fun of these devout Christians, calling them all kinds of names — 'the Holy Club', the 'the Bible Moths' and so forth. The nickname that stuck, and which John Wesley cheerfully accepted, was 'the Methodists' — a reference to their similarity to an earlier sect of Puritans so nicknamed because they had a method of theology.

John Wesley (1703–1791), charismatic leader of the Methodists. Along with his brother Charles, the hymn-writer, John Wesley did much to encourage ordinary people to 'sing lustily'.

The dedication of these Methodists was such that they sought to serve the wider community. In 1735 both John and Charles Wesley set sail for the American colonies to work as missionaries in Georgia. During the voyage they experienced terrible storms. John Wesley recorded in his *Journal* how, when he feared for his life, he had been impressed by the calm of the Moravian Christians on board, who in the midst of the storms, sang confident hymns to keep their spirits up. When they landed in Georgia one of the first things he did was to compile the first Methodist hymn book, which included his own translations of German hymns.

When John Wesley eventually returned from America, regarding his missionary work as something of a failure, he kept in touch with the Moravians, who invited him to a little meeting in Aldersgate Street, London. In his *Journal* he records how it was at this meeting, on the 24th May 1738, at 8.45pm, that he felt his heart 'strangely warmed' with a depth of faith and clearer vision that he had known before. His brother Charles had a similar spiritual experience a few days later, and celebrated the occasion by writing a hymn which typified the evangelistic spirit of Methodism — an attempt to reach, not church-goers, but the vast numbers of those who, as we would say today, were marginalised by society:

> Outcasts of men, to you I call!
> Harlots and publicans and thieves!
> He spreads his arms to embrace you all;
> Sinners alone his grace receives ...

This evangelistic fervour soon led to John Wesley's famous work as an open-air preacher, starting amongst the coalminers of Kingswood near Bristol in 1739, where another Oxford Methodist, George Whitfield, had already preached to the crowds with tremendous response.

By the time he died, in 1791, John Wesley had evangelised the whole of the British Isles, travelling an estimated 250,000 miles mostly on horseback, and preaching some 40,000 sermons often in the open air. When we add to this his pioneering social work — the founding of Kingswood School (still flourishing), the opening of two orphanages, the setting up of free dispensaries of medicine, the printing of all kinds of paperback Christian literature — it is not surprising that it has been claimed by certain historians that John Wesley saved the country, almost single-handed, from the equivalent of the French Revolution.

The Hymns of Methodism

The spectacular work of John Wesley in establishing the influential denomination of Methodism — originally a movement intended to revive the Church of England — was greatly helped by the work of his younger brother Charles. Though travelling around far less than John, and mostly leading the life of a settled Anglican vicar, Charles Wesley nevertheless supplied an essential component — the hymns the converts of Methodism needed to express their new found faith and commitment.

'Methodism was born in song'. These are the opening words of the preface to the first modern *Methodist Hymn Book,* published in 1933, when the various divisions of Methodism (notably the Wesleyans and the Primitive Methodists) had united as the Methodist Church. This hymn book also contains the preface written by John Wesley to his *Collection of Hymns for the People Called Methodists,* published in 1780, containing 525 hymns. In this he wittily protests against the plagiarism and alteration of his hymns:

> Many Gentlemen have done my Brother and me (though without naming us) the honour to reprint many of our hymns. Now they are perfectly welcome to do so, provided they print them just as they are. But I desire they would not attempt to mend them — for they really are not able. Therefore I must beg of them one of these two favours: either to let them stand just as they are ... or to add the true reading in the margin, or at the bottom of the page, that we may no longer be accountable either for the nonsense or the doggerel of other men.

Disregard for copyright also applied to the tunes, and these were borrowed, altered and set to different words almost indiscriminately. By the time our hymn tune was being used for *On Ilkla Mooar baht 'at* it had been set to half a dozen different hymns in a variety of hymn books published both here and in America.

In the *Methodist Hymn Book* and Methodism's *Hymns and Psalms* (1983) there are far more hymns by Charles Wesley than by any other writer — and this is true of hymn books of most other denominations. This is not surprising. Charles Wesley was a prolific poet, eventually writing as many as 7,000 hymns on every conceivable Christian topic. It is not, however, the quantity and variety which have made his hymns so popular and enduring. It is the superb quality of the language — its combination of strength and elegance, its skilful use of biblical doctrine and imagery, its original and memorable phrasing ... above all the way the warmth of feeling — what the Wesleys called 'the religion of the heart' — is conveyed by mere words.

These powerful new hymns of Charles Wesley required a new kind of music. The staid and solemn hymn tunes of the past were no longer appropriate. The tune of the old metrical psalms associated with Calvin, or the chorales associated with Luther, many used by Bach, had a wonderful dignity, but something more lively was needed for the singing of a typical Charles Wesley hymn such as the one beginning:

> O Thou who camest from above,
> The pure celestial fire to impart,
> Kindle a flame of sacred love
> On the mean altar of my heart!

The words alone give an idea of the nature of Methodist hymn-singing. It looks back to the Pentecostal fire of the Holy Spirit. It is never timid or mumbling or funereal, but the outward expression of a passionate inward faith. In the early years there were no musical instruments to accompany the singing — or enough hymn books for all the congregation. Indeed, many of the early Methodists being illiterate, the preacher would read out the words, two lines at a time. As Methodism developed, hymns became more and more popular, and tunes were specially composed or borrowed and adapted, so that words and music together gave the characteristic rousing hymns of Methodism.

The tradition that Methodists should throw off their inhibitions, break free from the restraints of a formal church service to the liberty of the open air or a country chapel and have a good sing, can be traced back to John Wesley's own approach to worship. Always somewhat High Church, and believing that worship should be orderly and dignified, he nevertheless encouraged his followers to put heart and soul into their singing, as in his directions for the use of the tune-book he published in 1761, *Sacred Melody*. These include a comment which would certainly have been heeded by the first singers of the tune to which *On Ilkla Mooar* is set:

> Sing *lustily*, and with a good courage. Beware of singing as if you were half dead or half asleep; but lift up your voice with strength. Be no more afraid of your voice now, nor more ashamed of its being heard, than when you sang the songs of Satan.

This reference to the worldly songs his converts had once sung in the taverns — 'the songs of Satan' — reminds us of the comment said to have been made by William Booth, originally a Methodist, founder of the Salvation Army: 'Why should the Devil have all the best tunes?' (Probably quoting the Rev Rowland Hill.) Some of the finest composers of classical music did occasionally write hymn tunes. Handel, for example, wrote three tunes for Charles Wesley's hymns, the best-known of which is 'Gopsal' for 'Rejoice! The Lord is King!' A similarly triumphant tune by Handel is the one he wrote in his oratorio *Judas Maccabaeus* for 'See, the conquering hero comes!', which all denominations now use for the appropriate hymn 'Thine be the glory, risen, conquering Son!'. Eventually Methodists were singing one of Charles Wesley's hymns to an aria from Mozart's *Magic Flute* — still one of the most popular in the hymn book, though few realise its origin.

This occasional movement of tunes from the secular world to the Church has gone almost without comment. In the case of *On Ilkla Mooar*, however, we have a rare example of movement in the opposite direction. What was originally a sacred melody has ended up as what Wesley would have called one of 'the songs of Satan'.

The Boot and Shoe Composer

The hymn-singing Methodists we considered in the last chapter had a strong following in the Kentish city of Canterbury, long famous as a religious centre, with its great cathedral founded in AD 597 by St Augustine and the shrine of Thomas Becket, murdered in 1170. The four assassins, incidentally, established an early if sinister connection with Yorkshire, because they fled north to take refuge in Knaresborough Castle, where the very dogs refused to eat the scraps of food which fell from their table.

As the composer of what is generally assumed to be a Yorkshire tune was, in fact, a Canterbury Methodist, let us now look at his background.

Methodism in Canterbury

John Wesley seems to have been especially drawn to Canterbury, visiting the city more than most other places in the kingdom. In his *Journal* he records that he stayed here or broke his journey, mostly to preach, on no less than thirty-nine occasions. The first visit was on the 29th January 1750, when he preached in the evening — and again at five o'clock the next morning, following his normal custom of getting up at four am. On this first visit he noted in his *Journal* that he hoped the people of Canterbury would worship God with 'more knowledge and as much earnestness' as their forefathers had venerated Thomas Becket. On his next visit in the following December he found some of his congregation rather noisy. The next day he looked round the cathedral and at the monuments and tombs of the famous. He was not impressed. All had been reduced to dust, he noted. 'Where are the great, the fair, the valiant now? The matchless warrior, the puissant monarch?'

Wesley's concern, as always, was with the ordinary working folk, including the soldiers stationed in Canterbury. In 1756 he spoke to a number of men and their officers, and was invited to dine with their colonel, and on a later visit preached to 200 soldiers and a row of officers. The presence of the military was often needed in those unruly times, especially when Methodist preachers were attacked by hostile mobs. John Wesley does not seem to have been physically attacked there as he was elsewhere, but on the 16th October 1758, as he was riding into Canterbury, 'a stone flew out of the pavement' striking his horse on the leg, causing it to fall and roll over on top of him, injuring his right thigh. A barber who saw the accident carried him into his shop, and looked after him.

Two years later Wesley noted that the congregations of Methodists in Canterbury were 'larger than I ever remember', and on the 20th August 1764 he preached at the opening of the new chapel, which had been built from the old stones of St Andrew's Church, pulled down the previous year. Though numerous, always filling the chapel to overflowing, the Canterbury Methodists were, in 1765, reported to Wesley as having 'fallen from grace' — but he personally found nothing to criticise, and always seems to have enjoyed his visits, describing his stay here as 'comfortable' or as having given him 'much satisfaction', especially when he had the leisure to read or visit his friends the Perronet brothers. These were Huguenots, connected with a congregation of French refugees who met in the crypt of Canterbury Cathedral, later in the Malthouse, where Wesley preached. One of the brothers, Edward Perronet, wrote the hymn 'All hail the power of Jesu's name!'

Wesley's work in Canterbury provided a firm foundation for the fast-growing Methodist movement. In 1791, the year John Wesley died, there were 296 Methodist members in Canterbury. By 1815 the membership had grown to 570. Most of them would have come from an Anglican background, as did Thomas Clark, the composer with whom we are concerned. His grandfather, also called Thomas, was parish clerk of St Peter's. This man's fourth son, William, became a cordwainer, a maker of boots and shoes. He also became a Methodist — perhaps converted, or at least influenced, by the preaching of John Wesley. He brought up his first son as a Methodist, naming him Thomas, after his father.

Thomas Clark (1775-1859)

William Clark, having served his apprenticeship and having become a freeman of Canterbury in 1771, married Mary Quested in 1774, and began to sell his own boots and shoes from Clark's Boot Shop, 35 St George's Street, the site now occupied by part of Marks and Spencer. It was over the boot and shoe shop here that Thomas Clark was born, being baptised in St Peter's Church on the 5th February 1775.

The boy grew up in a musical household. William Clark, his father, was not only a keen supporter of the Methodist chapel, but a member of the choir and then its choirmaster, mainly at the new St Peter's Chapel, opened in 1811. The Canterbury Methodists at this time were very progressive. Whereas John Wesley had in his

St Peter's Methodist Chapel, Canterbury (1811), where Thomas Clark was choirmaster, like his father before him.

five published collections of hymn tunes envisaged accompaniment by the harpsichord or organ, most hymns were still sung unaccompanied. Even in 1805 the Methodist Conference decreed that the only instrument permitted during services was a bass viol, and the following year Conference went so far as to ban organs as being alien to the simplicity of Methodist services. In Canterbury, however, the singing was accompanied by a small orchestra, in which one of Thomas Clark's uncles — apparently a very stout man — played a kind of wind equivalent of the bass viol, a serpent.

Wallace Harvey's research on Thomas Clark showed that this chapel orchestra practised in a room at the back of the shop, just underneath the bedroom of little Thomas Clark, often keeping him awake. For any lack of sleep he received ample compensation in the interest this evoked in music. From an early age he was regularly taken by his father to the choir practices, becoming familiar both with hymn tunes and more ambitious works such as Handel's *Messiah*, composed in 1742. Early Methodism frowned on anthems and oratorios, insisting that congregational singing should have priority. But in 1758 John Wesley heard a performance of *Messiah* in Bristol Cathedral, and was greatly impressed. By the end of the eighteenth century, especially amongst more enterprising Methodists like those at Canterbury, it was being performed by ordinary choirs — in chapels as well as cathedrals. One of the most appealing of the traditions collected by Wallace Harvey is that, when only a little boy, Thomas Clark stood on a chair to conduct Handel's *Messiah*.

Nor was this just an indulgence to humour a child who wanted to play at conducting in imitation of his father. Thomas, though by no means a prodigy, had real musical talent. It is said that when very young he composed hymn tunes, and that long before he could read or write — which was not, in fact, till he was a young man — he was able to read and write music, no doubt tutored in this by his father.

It may seem surprising that a father who was competent enough to direct performances of *Messiah* should not have paid more attention to his son's education. Yet the Clarks were typical of early Methodist musicians who were so often drawn from the ranks of artisans and ordinary working folk. Music to them was not associated with a privileged education, but with the expression of their faith — the combination of inspiration and musical gifts resulting in many a good hymn tune being composed by working men rather than by a professional, highly-trained musician. There is even a parallel to Thomas Clark in the Lancashire shoemaker John Fawcett (1789-1867), who was a self-taught musician, composer of hymns and organist at a Wesleyan Chapel in Bolton. Though the theatre and opera, dancing and the reading of novels, were in general shunned by Methodists, music — so closely linked with religion — was the one great source of cultural pleasure. And it could go hand-in-hand with manual work, in this case the craft of the cordwainer.

We can assume that William Clark was less concerned that his son should read and write than that he should follow him in his own trade and eventually inherit his business. Thomas, apprenticed to his father, learnt how to work in leather and make boots and shoes, completing his apprenticeship in 1796 at the age of twenty-one, when he became, like his father before him, a freeman of Canterbury. His mother did not live to see it, having died two years earlier at the age of fifty-five. His father married again, this time to a much younger woman, Hannah Newman, the marriage taking place in St George's Church, which was just opposite the shop. In little over a year this second marriage came to a sad end in the death of Hannah at the age of thirty-seven.

Thomas Clark found a release from the sorrows of the household, and the labour of making and selling footwear, by developing his talent for music. He had an interest in bell-ringing and went round to many churches in the district to offer his assistance as a ringer. It was, however, as conductor of hymn-singing that he soon earned a reputation, and it is evident that he had been apprenticed to his father as a trainee conductor no less than as a trainee boot and shoe maker.

Cranbrook, in the heart of the Weald, Kent, is still dominated by the biggest working smock mill in England, dating from 1814, which would have been familiar to Thomas Clark.

Along with his conducting went the exploitation of hymn tunes he had composed himself, and which he was now in an ideal position to try out and promote. His favourite place for this was in the market town of Cranbrook, where he was invited to conduct the large choir of Shepherds House School, having been befriended by the headmaster, John Francis.

The kind of setting in which Clark's hymns would later be sung is illustrated in the fine painting by Thomas Webster RA, *The Village Choir*, exhibited at the Royal Academy in 1847. As Webster became the leader of the 'Cranbrook Colony' of artists, it has been wrongly assumed that this painting shows Cranbrook Church. It is in fact Bow Brickhill Church in Buckinghamshire. According to Wallace Harvey, a family tradition claimed that the conductor in the picture was John Francis, and that the man playing the clarinet was Thomas Clark. But there is no evidence that the painter visited Cranbrook before 1853 — and even in 1847 Clark would have been seventy-two. Webster could have used an earlier portrait by another artist, but this seems unlikely, and we have no authenticated picture of the composer.

The Francis family in general gave great encouragement to the young composer and persuaded him to publish his increasingly

A Set of
Psalm & Hymn Tunes
with some SELECT PIECES and an
Anthem,
COMPOSED IN A FAMILIAR STYLE
and Figured for the
ORGAN, PIANO FORTE &c.
By Thos. Clark, Canterbury.
Entd at Statrs Hall. — LONDON — Price Five Shills
Printed by Button, Whitaker, & Beadnell, 75, St. Paul's Church Yard.

Title page from Thomas Clark's first Set of Psalm and Hymn Tunes *(1805), containing the first printed version of 'Cranbrook' (no 20) and costing five shillings.*

The Village Choir *(1847) by Thomas Webster RA, leader of the 'Cranbrook Colony' of artists. This oil painting vividly portrays the kind of setting in which the tune of* On Ilkla Mooar *would first have been sung. It has been stated that the composer Thomas Clark is the man playing the clarinet, but there is no historical evidence to support this.* (Courtesy of the Trustees of the Victoria and Albert Museum)

popular hymn tunes so they could reach a wider, even national, audience. So in 1805 Thomas Clark published the first of seven collections of his hymn tunes. Engraved by James Peck and printed in London by Button, Whitaker and Beadnell of St Paul's Church Yard, it is entitled *A Set of Psalm and Hymn Tunes*. Scored for 'organ, piano forte etc' it consists of an anthem and twenty-seven tunes, the most interesting of which bears the significant name of 'Cranbrook'.

The Tune called 'Cranbrook'

Of all his early compositions, this tune must have been one that Thomas Clark felt especially pleased with. The town of Cranbrook

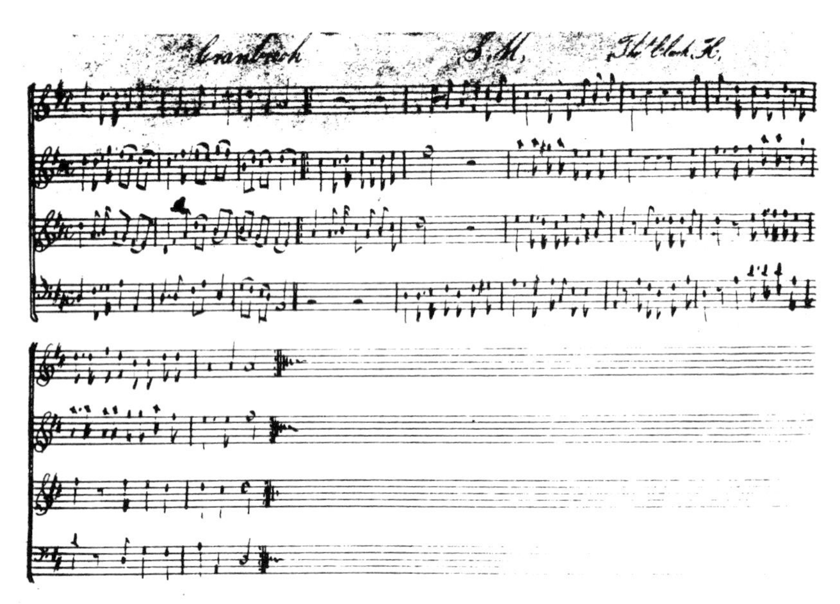

The original manuscript of the hymn tune 'Cranbrook', signed by Thomas Clark. The melody is the third line down, sung by the tenors.

had come to mean so much to him, not simply because he had a good relationship with the school choir, but because the friendship of the master, John Francis, extended to his having taught Clark — at long last — to read and write. This crowning achievement came at the age of twenty-eight, just two years before he published his first collection of hymns. I think we can reasonably assume that he wrote the tune he called 'Cranbrook' in gratitude to John Francis and, in particular, to celebrate his belated arrival at literacy.

It was, of course, not unusual to name a hymn tune after a place with personal associations. Wallace Harvey has explained the origin of some of the other names in Clark's first collection of hymns. 'St Peter's', for example, is named after the church linked with the family before they became Methodists, and 'Rose Lane', he says, is named after a little lane — since destroyed in the Blitz — which once joined their own street of St George's. 'Burham' was named after the seaside town in Essex while Clark was staying at the home of one of the Francis girls at Great Walkering — apparently after a contest with her brother, Jabez Francis, to see who could compose a hymn tune quickest. Quite apart from its personal associations with the composer, the attractive Kent market town of Cranbrook well deserves to be celebrated in a world-famous melody.

Although 'Cranbrook' was published in the 1805 collection, it would have been composed a year or two before — perhaps in 1803, the year Clark learnt to read and write. His autograph manuscript of the time bears no date, but he certainly could write by this time, as we see from the title, 'S.M.' (Short Metre) and the composer's signature, all written in a fair hand, as is the music in four parts in the key of two sharps.

The first words to be sung to 'Cranbrook' were those of the hymn by Philip Doddridge, 'Grace, 'tis a charming sound'. Doddridge was not a Methodist, but strongly supported the work of the Wesley brothers, and was visited by John Wesley at the Nonconformist academy of which he was principal in Northampton. He had considerable influence, especially through his hymns, which followed those of Isaac Watts as a contribution to Independent hymnology. Amongst his best-known are the dignified advent hymn 'Hark the glad sound!', and one which anticipates modern choruses, 'O happy day that fixed my choice!'

The word 'grace' used by Doddridge in the 'Cranbrook' hymn is a theological term connected with the emphasis of the evangelical revival on the nature of salvation — not something earned by good works, but freely available to the believer through the atoning work of Christ, a forgiveness made possible through the grace of God. To express this Christian sense of gratitude for the 'grace' — the undeserved generosity — of God, a hymn tune was needed that had both dignity and a sense of joyous thanksgiving. 'Cranbrook' seemed to be exactly what was required as, from 1805, they began to sing the original of what eventually became *On Ilkla Mooar*:

> Grace, 'tis a charming Sound,
> Harmonious to mine Ear;

Heav'n with the Echo shall resound,
And all the Earth shall hear!

At first sight the words of the first line do not fit the tune — and only work if 'charming' is sung over four notes, but Thomas Clark seemed happy with the setting, and in later life he is remembered as having urged the choirs he conducted to give all their strength to the triumphant last line, repeated — as in the modern song — three times.

What, I imagine, must have had a special appeal was the way the third line, 'Heaven with the echo shall resound', is quite literally echoed by the basses in the choir, before the whole choir takes the hymn to its climax.

As a Methodist, delighted with the incomparable hymns of Charles Wesley, I may be accused of prejudice, but the Doddridge hymn as a whole is one of his weakest and it is not surprising that it is rarely sung today. It was, however, wedded to 'Cranbrook', and this guaranteed its popularity well into the late Victorian period, when it was said to be the favourite hymn of the great Baptist preacher C H Spurgeon.

Now they were in print, the hymn tunes of Thomas Clark were being used everywhere, especially 'Cranbrook'. It was soon realised that it was an ideal fuguing tune for exuberant words such as those in the well-known Charles Wesley hymn:

O for a thousand tongues to sing
My great Redeemer's praise,
The glories of my God and King,
The triumphs of His grace!

It is interesting to note that another popular choice for this hymn was the tune 'Lyngham', published in about 1803, a little earlier than 'Cranbrook'. This has a similar lively style, with the last line sung three times. 'Lyngham' was composed by the Baptist, Thomas Jarman, born in a Northamptonshire village just a year later than Thomas Clark in 1776. Like him he was a tradesman, in this case a tailor, like his father before him, but his musical ability took over and, as a contemporary of Clark, he composed and published his own hymn tunes.

As 'Cranbrook' now spread to various denominations and their hymn books, other words were sung to it. As well as those by Charles Wesley, there was, for example, the hymn by Isaac Watts, 'Come, ye that love the Lord'. In Kent and elsewhere, but especially in Yorkshire, it was a popular choice at Christmas for 'While Shepherds watched their flocks by night'.

Clark as Choirmaster

The publication of Clark's first *Set of Psalm and Hymn Tunes* in 1805, as well as his personal contacts, led to success as a choirmaster, not simply conducting the choir of his own chapel, St Peter's, in Canterbury, as his father had done, but going round to direct choirs of other churches, such as that of Cranbrook Parish Church, and united Methodist choirs on special occasions like Sunday school anniversaries and the opening of chapels. He must have been aware of the upset at the St Peter's Chapel caused by the frivolous behaviour of some of those in the singing gallery in 1816. This led to the Methodists making various resolutions concerning their musicians and singers, such as 'No person shall be admitted into the orchestra or as a singer who lives in habitual, open sin ... No person shall be permitted to retain his seat in the orchestra whose behaviour is irreverent during divine service.'

Thomas Clark, in addition to his peripatetic conducting, was now becoming a prolific composer, following the *Second Set of Psalm and Hymn Tunes* (1806) with a more ambitious collection 'with Symphonies and Instrumental Bass, adapted for the use of Parish or County Choirs and figured for the Organ etc'. By 1820 he had produced his *Seventh Set of Hymn Tunes* and was beginning to be known for his anthems, as well as his hymns. Perhaps his most important contribution to church music was when in 1837 he was invited by the Sunday School Union to compile a collection published as *The Union Tune Book*. This contained 319 hymn tunes, 38 of them by Clark, including his most popular composition, 'Cranbrook'.

His book is prefaced by an 'Introduction to Singing' which indicates how seriously and professionally the singing of hymns was approached in those days:

> To produce full, mellow tones, the sound should proceed freely from the chest, and the mouth be opened moderately, with the appearance of a smile ... Practise the sounds of the notes in the scale, both ascending and descending, as far as the voice can be extended without forcing it. Let the voice dwell firmly on each sound ... gradually increase the sound till the middle, and then decrease until it die away. By thus practising the sounds in the scale, which many do while at their daily occupations, the voice will be materially strengthened and improved.

After stressing the importance of the words, always to be pronounced distinctly and accurately, the manner and technique of the singers is examined:

> All such bad habits as singing through the nose, distorting the face, beginning lines abruptly, making a loud noise, taking breath in the middle of a word, and dwelling too long on the last note, are very disagreeable, and ought to be carefully avoided.

Then there is a plea for the making of marriages between words and music which would certainly have been exemplified by 'Cranbrook' in most of its settings:

> The persons who lead the singing should be careful to select tunes adapted to the words. A hymn expressive of joy and praise ought to be set to a tune of the same character.

The Union Tune Book proved extremely popular, becoming a standard work amongst Nonconformists, and was followed by several editions and other works, such as *The Union Harmonist* (1841) and a hymn book for Sunday school children, *The Juvenile Harmonist*

'Cranbrook' as it appeared in the influential Union Tune Book, *first published in 1837, and edited by Thomas Clark for the Sunday School Union.*

(1842). The following year Clark published *The Seraphim, or Sacred Harmonist*, a collection of tunes and anthems, including his own. His anthems were of a high order. The hymnologist J T Lightwood noted that Clark's anthem *Daughter of Zion* 'achieved an extraordinary popularity, and the crashing chord at the end of the phrase "chariots of war" is ever a joyful memory to those who have heard or sung it'. There is no doubt that Clark was greatly esteemed as a church musician, his tunes turning up in all kinds of hymn books, such as the *Lyra Sacra* (1840) in whose preface we see him singled out:

> Here are some of the best tunes by the best masters of music, and those by Clark of Canterbury, though last, are not the least in excellence of composition.

A measure of the esteem in which Clark is still held was the formation in 1992 of the Kent-based Thomas Clark Quire, a popular group of twenty singers and musicians who perform early hymns and psalms, including those of Clark.

Towards the end of his life Clark resigned from St Peter's Methodist chapel — probably because he was suspected of holding

Unitarian views — and joined the General Baptists at the Black Friars. Long after retirement from the boot and shoe trade, he continued to conduct choirs all over the Canterbury district at anniversaries, funerals and evening 'sings' of massed choirs, sometimes travelling around in a friend's dog-cart.

Thomas Clark died, aged eighty-four, on the 30th May 1859. We can be fairly sure that he did not live to see the adoption of his favourite tune 'Cranbrook' as a dialect song. He is buried in Wincheap Burial Ground, Canterbury. Would he turn in his grave if he knew? Or would be be gratified to know that this curious secularisation of his tune has helped to take his music all round the world?

Introducing Yorkshire Dialect

For a minority of older Yorkshire readers, the county's dialect needs no introduction. They remember the days when the language used in *On Ilkla Mooar* was part of the everyday speech of ordinary working people. For the majority, unsure of what the words in the song mean and how they should be pronounced, I will say something about what Yorkshire dialect is and how it originated.

It is, in fact, only when we put the curious words of the song into their historical context that we can appreciate that they are not a specially-contrived kind of comic language, like some linguistic gimmick, but far more ordinary than they first may seem, arising out of a colloquial style that was once natural and normal. This is something I can testify to myself, because I grew up in an area of the West Riding where language of the kind used in the song surrounded my early years. As a result the words have never seemed to me in the least quaint, but simply the older, distinctive Yorkshire speech I heard — and sometimes used — as a boy.

Our Disappearing Dialect

The words of *On Ilkla Mooar* are essentially a survival from an earlier age — though by no means as early as 1805, when the music first appeared. We have to make an effort to adjust to the words because this kind of dialect is so rarely heard today, and authentic speakers of it are what I would regard as an endangered species — few and far between, talking dialect amongst themselves, but usually adopting something more like Standard English when talking to **off-comed-uns**.

There are, of course, many people who speak with a strong Yorkshire accent and intonation, with both the vowels and the rise and fall of the voice clearly marking them out as Yorkshire. But local accent and intonation — what we in the Yorkshire Dialect Society would call 'regional speech' — is by no means the same as the dialect in which it has its origins. True dialect includes special items of vocabulary — words never used in Standard English, or not used in the same way — and also its own idioms and sayings, mostly incomprehensible to speakers from other areas.

The reason for the gradual erosion of genuine dialect is — as we shall see — fairly complex, but there is no doubt that dialect has long been regarded with prejudice by people who have confused it with slang and slovenly English. True, the 'h' is automatically dropped (but so it is in French), along with the final 'g', and there are some forms which look grammatically incorrect, but which have, in fact, a long ancestry.

It is also true that the image of dialect has not been helped by well-intentioned but largely bogus attempts to reintroduce it — the kind of word-lists and booklets which include general slang, and incorrect and untypical words and phrases, grotesquely spelt, giving the impression that Yorkshire dialect is a comical novelty, merely good for a giggle.

The fact is, though, that — far from being a corrupted or eccentric kind of English — real dialect is an ancient and honorable form of speech, with its roots deep in the language of the Angles, Vikings and Normans, and a strength and subtlety of expression all of its own.

The term 'broad Yorkshire' is a comparatively recent one. The earliest reference I can find is to Yorkshire itself — the biggest county in England — as a county of 'broad acres'. The same adjective — perhaps by coincidence — then seems to have been applied to the vowels of Yorkshire speech, which are 'broad' in the sense that they are full, pure and unrounded — all derived from the ancient speech of the nations we shall now consider.

The Language of the Angles

Yorkshire dialect had its first roots in the language of people who gave their name to England, literally the 'land of the Angles'.

Though often confused with the Saxons, the latter settled further south, as can be seen in names like Essex (named after the East Saxons), Sussex (South Saxons) etc. The difference between the speech of the Angles in the north and the Saxons in the south was sufficient to give a basis to the difference between northern and southern English — though we describe their language in general as Anglo-Saxon or Old English.

The Angles came here in the middle of the fifth century, soon after the occupying Roman forces had withdrawn. They came from the northern part of Germany we now call Schleswig-Holstein, bringing with them a Germanic speech, which explains why we can still see resemblances between Yorkshire dialect and modern German.

Notice, first, that many of the vowels are short. For example, dialect **finnd** instead of 'find' (cf German *finden*), **brokken** instead of 'broken' (cf German *gebrochen*) If our Anglian ancestors were to return they would feel more at home with the short vowels of Yorkshire dialect than the longer ones of Standard English — in words like **fatther, mutther, oppen, frozzen, telled, etten** etc.

Not only does dialect often retain the pronunciation of the Angles, but sometimes vocabulary which still resembles German. For example, the verb **sam** in the phrase **sam it up!** (pick it up) is the Anglian word *samnian* (cf German *sammeln*) meaning 'to gather, collect'. Best known of all is the use of the word **starve**, which in Yorkshire dialect can refer to suffering because of intense cold, as in the phrase like **Ah wor fair starved aht theeare**. It was once so common that it was used by speakers who did not normally use dialect, such as Cathy in *Wuthering Heights*, who at one point in the novel says 'Ellen, shut the window. I'm starving!' Though puzzling to readers who might wonder why she should want the window shut because she was ravenously hungry, **starve** here is not an ignorant misuse, but simply the original Anglo-Saxon verb *steorfan*, which literally means 'to die' (cf German *starb*) used in the sense of intense suffering, because you can perish from cold as well as from hunger.

A similar derivative from Anglo-Saxon is that odd word in the opening line of our song, **baht**, from *be-utan*, meaning 'without'. This is not to say that the words of *Ilkla Mooar* are simply Anglo-Saxon, but they are closer to it than any modern English song would be, and our Anglian ancestors would have found the words easier to sing and understand than many a resident of contemporary Yorkshire.

Mercia versus Northumbria

It is important to realise that there is not simply one uniform Yorkshire dialect, but that it varies very considerably, as we might expect in a county so big that it has more acres (3,923,359) than letters in the King James's Bible (3,566,840). You can travel from

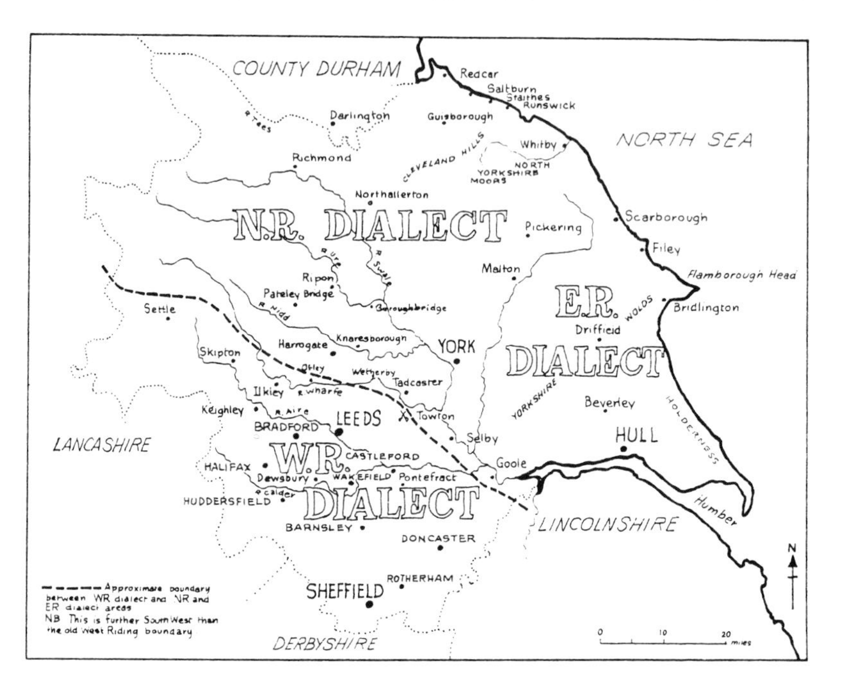

Map of the dialect areas (from the author's Yorkshire Dictionary*).*

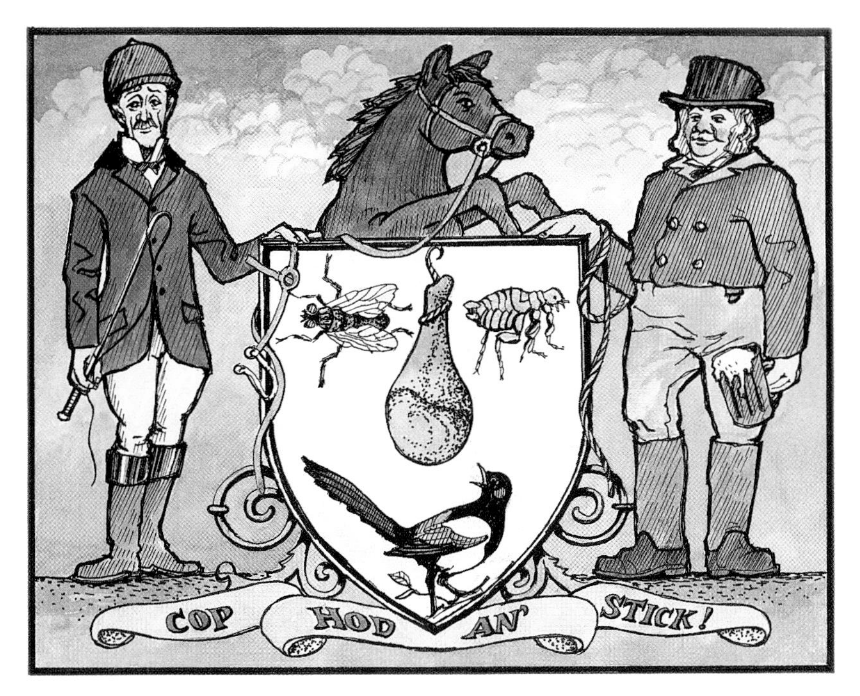

The Yorkshireman's 'coat of arms', an early example of blunt, leg-pulling humour. (Peter Kearney)

one valley to another — even from one village to another — and find a difference in the local speech.

There are two main divisions of Yorkshire dialect, arising from the fact that the Angles were subdivided — in addition to East Anglia — into two great kingdoms, each with its own style of speech. These were Northumbria — originally all the territory north of the River Humber — and Mercia, roughly the Midlands and part of what we now call the West Riding.

There is still a marked difference between Mercian speech, the basis of West Riding dialect, and Northumbrian speech, the basis of North Riding and East Riding dialect. The two groups have much in common, of course, and at meetings of the Yorkshire

Dialect Society we always understand each other and enjoy listening to the other style of speech, though it can take some time to become attuned to the difference in vowels, as these examples will show:

	West Riding	*North and East Ridings*
down	**dahn**	**doon**
boot	**booit**	**beeat**
speak	**speyk**	**speeak**
none	**nooan**	**neean**
coat	**coit**	**cooat**
home	**'ooame**	**yam**

The northernmost limit of West Riding speech, incidentally, is not the old West Riding boundary, but approximately along the valley of the Wharfe, extending a little towards Nidderdale.

I would say that the most striking difference between the two major dialect areas is that North and East Riding dialect — being from a largely rural area — is softer, more gentle, than West Riding dialect which tends to be spoken more loudly and more harshly — no doubt reflecting life in the industrial towns, when millions of millworkers really did have to develop the kind of speech that could be heard amidst the noise of the textile machinery.

The words of our song are unmistakably West Riding dialect, exactly the same kind of speech as we find, for example, in the so-called 'Yorkshireman's Motto', said with tongue-in-cheek wry humour:

> **'Ear all, see all, say nowt;**
> **Eyt all, sup all, pay nowt,**
> **An' if ivver tha does owt fer nowt**
> **Do it fer thissen!**

Notice that in most parts of Yorkshire, **owt** and **nowt** are pronounced with the diphthong 'aw-oo', not to rhyme with 'now'. Notice also the use of the familiar form **tha** (you) and **thissen** (yourself). Though the use of thou/thee has gone from modern English it is preserved in dialect, usually for speaking to one person who is a friend or member of the family — just as we have in German (*du* as distinct from *Sie*) and French (*tu* as distinct from *vous*). In some parts of the West Riding the thou/thee form is still used amongst close friends. It is worth knowing that you have to wait until someone chooses to address you as thou/thee before you can indulge in this intimacy yourself. You can easily make a social blunder by addressing somebody — in a pub, for example — as thou/thee if you have not yet been recognised as a friend — something we see summed up in the saying: '**Dooan't thee-tha *me*: Tha thee-tha's them 'at thee-tha's thee!**' Finally, notice that **tha** — which goes with **thee**, **thy** (or **thi**), **thine** and **thissen** — is very commonly reduced to **ta** (short 'a'), as in questions like '**What's ta doin'?**' and in the opening line of the song.

The Contribution of the Vikings

About four centuries after the Angles had settled in Yorkshire there was another invasion, this time from Scandinavia. First came the Danish Vikings, who captured York in AD 867 AD, changing its name from the Anglian Eorforvic to the more Danish-sounding Jorvik ('J' pronounced as 'Y', as in German). They also divided the vast county into three administrative areas which they called *thrith-jungr* (third part), a word which ended up as Riding.

A little later than the Danish Vikings — around 900 AD — the Norwegian Vikings or Norsemen moved from their settlement in Ireland into the Yorkshire Dales. Together the Vikings gave Scandinavian names to villages such as those ending in '-thwaite' or '-thorpe', to features of the countryside, such as beck, fell, ghyll, carr, foss etc, and to streets, especially Briggate (the way to the bridge) and Kirkgate (the way to the church). They also contributed their own words to the language of Yorkshire, many of which still survive in dialect, including **addle** (to earn), **stee** (ladder), **teem** (to pour), **kist** (wooden chest) — and **laik**, still the word for 'to play' in Scandinavian languages.

There is a Viking word in the opening question of the song —

bahn (going). This is an older West Riding form of modern English 'bound' (as in 'north-bound'), probably derived from Old Norse *buinn*. It could also be connected with Norwegian *bane* (track) or German *Bahn* (way, path). The link between 'bahn' and other languages is nicely illustrated by the story of the Yorkshire folk in Germany trying to ask the way to the station, but not knowing the German word. Having failed to get anybody to understand, one Yorkshireman, losing patience, started to walk away saying, '**Oh, Ah'm bahn off!**' 'Ah', said the Germans, 'Now we understand. You want the *Bahnhof* (station).'

1066 and All That

The last of the three invasions and settlements, that by the Normans, had less impact on Yorkshire dialect, but some of the Norman French words took their place alongside the English ones, giving useful pairs of meaning. There are well-known culinary examples such as English 'sheep' for the animal in the fields, but French 'mutton' (*le mouton*) for when it was meat on the table. The English 'room' was now accompanied by 'chamber' (French *la chambre*), which in Yorkshire dialect gave **cham'er** (bedroom). One of my favourite Yorkshire words is **buffit**. In Standard English we speak of a 'buffet meal', deriving this from the modern French word *le buffet*, which means 'sideboard'. Yorkshire dialect, however, preserves the original Norman French meaning of buffet — a low stool.

In spite of the fact that French was spoken by the Norman nobility, military, priests, administrators and so forth, it never managed to supplant Old English as the language of the people. Gradually the two languages — at first spoken in different circles — mingled until they produced Middle English. The process was completed by about 1400, the year of Chaucer's death, with roughly a third of the words now being of French origin.

There was still no official, standard language — only dialects. But after 1400 one of these dialects — the speech of the London area used by Chaucer and later printed by Caxton — began to spread, being taken all over the county by officials, merchants and educated people. It is not surprising that the kind of English used by the capital city began to impose itself on the rest of the country, making local dialects appear inferior to what eventually became Standard English with Received Pronunciation.

The war of attrition against dialect — sometimes a quite deliberate policy of elimination — took various forms. Mainly it was through education. Children who were taught to read and write were expected to pronounce words like all the others who could read and write. So in Yorkshire the short vowel in **fatther** and **watter**, for example, would be changed to the longer one in 'father' and 'water.' Moreover, many of the words used by children in everyday speech — words like **summat** and **nobbut**, for example — never appeared in print at all. The pressure to conform, to 'talk properly', was above all else the enemy of dialect.

In addition to the influence of teachers and parents, there were other reasons for the decline of dialect — the movement of workers to different parts of the county, the upward mobility of those seeking promotion and social betterment, and, in more recent times, the ease and rapidity of travel, the expansion of housing, accompanied with social mixing, and the influence of the media, especially radio and television.

The Resurgence of Dialect

Even by the eighteenth century it must have seemed only a matter of time before all dialects, and even local accents, were completely eliminated, with everybody speaking in similar style the printed English that had now become standard. But the speech of ordinary people usually proves to be remarkably resilient, with a built-in resistance to the imposition of conformity. In the second half of the eighteenth century there appeared that great champion of dialect, Robert Burns, who chose to write many of his poems and songs in the language of his native Ayrshire. Soon after the death of Burns (1796) his influence could be seen in those who were now compiling lists of dialect words or writing down dialect sayings, proverbs and songs.

Burns had drawn attention to the fact that ordinary dialect — which it had now become the fashion to despise — could be used to great effect, especially in the writing of verse. His fellow countryman, Sir Walter Scott (1771-1832), was fascinated by local colour and dialect, including that of Yorkshire, publishing a version he had collected of the ancient *Lyke Wake Dirge*. This, in North Riding dialect, was a funeral lament, in a way anticipating *On Ilkla Mooar*, though this was sung in deadly earnest as they carried the **lyke** (corpse) over the fells to its last resting place, the journey through the rough, prickly **whinnies** (gorse) being compared to the progress of the soul through purgatory:

> **This yah neet, this yah neet,**
> **Ivvery neet an' all,**
> **Fire an' fleet an' cann'l leet,**
> **An' Christ tak up thi saul.**

The grim dirge goes on to describe how the soul must pass over **t' Brig o' Dreead** (the Bridge of Dread). It may pass safely over, but if the person in life has given neither silver nor gold to the poor, the soul will fall from the bridge into the flames of Hell:

> **Bud if o' siller an' gawd thoo nivver ga' neean,**
> **Ivvery neet an' all,**
> **Thoo'll doon, doon tumm'le tiwards Hell fleeams,**
> **An' Christ tak up thi saul!**

As well as being introduced to folk songs like this, readers were now coming across Yorkshire dialect in novels, especially in Emily Brontë's *Wuthering Heights* (1847), where the old servant Joseph speaks such rich Haworth dialect that, in the edition published after Emily's death, Charlotte felt obliged to water it down to make it more comprehensible to readers, changing **dahn** to 'down', for example. Poets were now writing original dialect verse, some deliberately following the example of Burns, one Keighley poet William Wright, actually wearing Scots clothing and calling himself 'The Yorkshire Burns'.

Finally, dialect was reinstated as a language in its own right by the work of Professor Joseph Wright and the Yorkshire Dialect Society. Joe Wright started work at the age of six, leading a donkey cart in a quarry at Windhill, Shipley. At the age of fifteen, when working as a woolsorter at Salts Mill, he decided it was high time he learnt to read and write. Through outstanding determination and enterprise he worked his way through night school to college, eventually graduating at Heidelberg and ending up as professor of comparative philology at Oxford. Inspired by the love of his native Yorkshire dialect, he undertook his great work — the production of the English Dialect Dictionary, finally published in six volumes in 1905. In order to compile this, he set up committees all over the country, collecting dialect words. The one in Bradford, when it had completed its work in 1897, decided to continue as the Yorkshire Dialect Society, which is now the longest-surviving dialect society in the world, still actively promoting interest in the traditional dialects of Yorkshire.

The real resurgence of Yorkshire dialect, however, was not amongst those with an academic or creative interest, but amongst ordinary working people. Long before Joseph Wright and the YDS, there had arisen that remarkable phenomenon — the real sociological context in which *On Ilkla Mooar* should be set — the dialect almanack.

The Dialect Almanacks

The proof that Yorkshire dialect was being spoken and enjoyed on a wide scale throughout most of the nineteenth century can be seen in the dialect almanacks — originally annual booklets containing a calendar, dates of notable events, phases of the moon etc, in the tradition of *Old Moore's Almanack*, but in Yorkshire with items in dialect. The dialect content — both prose and verse — was so popular that it increased to the point where the almanacks were almost entirely devoted to it, thus providing working people with a cheap printed version of the language most of them habitually spoke or understood, but which had previously only appeared in occasional books by poets or academics.

The dialect almanack was a product of the industrial West Riding, read almost exclusively by people whose living depended on the mines, mills and steel foundries. The first to appear were in Sheffield, the *Wheelswarf Chronicle* (1830) and the *Shevvild Chap's Annual* (1836), both edited by the Sheffield steelworker and dialect poet Abel Bywater. Then in Barnsley we had the *Barnsla Fooakes' Annual an' Pogmoor Olmenack*, edited by 'Tom Treddlehoyle' (Charles Rogers), which first appeared in 1843 and ran till the end of the century.

In the second half of the nineteenth century the almanacks gathered momentum, populous cities like Leeds supporting two, *T' Frogland Olmenac an' Leeds Loiners Annual* (from 1852) and *Tommy Toddles's Comic Almenack* (from 1862). Between 1870 and 1881, eighteen different almanacks were being published in the West Riding, the most northerly and the only one outside the industrial area being *T' Nidderdill Olminac*, published at Pateley Bridge from 1886.

Best-known of all was the one published in the heart of the area most closely associated with *On Ilkla Mooar*, the famous *Clock Almanack*, published in Halifax from 1865 and running until as recently as 1957, by which time it was being published in Bradford. It was founded by a Halifax hatter, John Wilson, who named it after the illuminated clock on the front of his shop — *The Original Illuminated Clock Almanack*. From 1867 until his death — a period of almost fifty years — it was edited by the lively and prolific dialect writer John Hartley, a Halifax weaver, who had the rare ability to celebrate the life of working class people in their own language. Through the eyes of Hartley, we can see in both dialect prose and verse the humour and hardship of life in the industrial West Riding. The fact that Hartley wrote most of the material himself, and also gave immensely popular public recitations in dialect, led to the

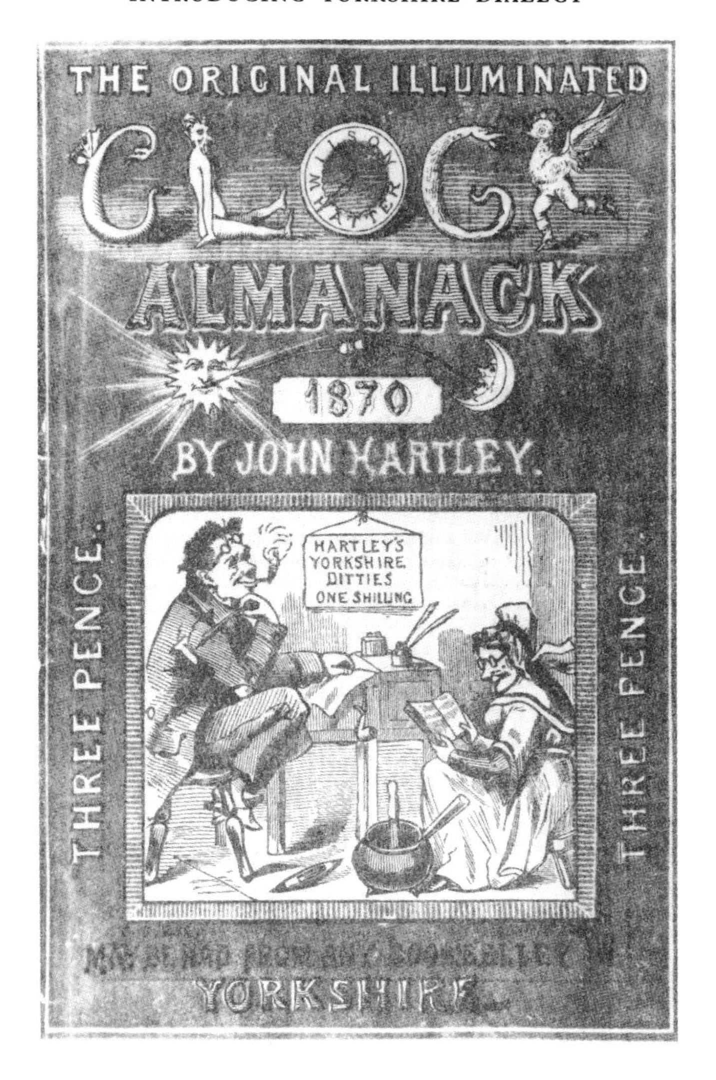

One of the Victorian issues of John Hartley's Clock Almanack, *whose dialect contents would have been enjoyed by the singers of* On Ilkla Mooar.

Clock becoming the most successful publication of its kind, selling as many as 120,000 copies a year.

In addition to editing the almanack and giving his dialect performances, John Hartley published several collections of his work, notably *Yorkshire Lyrics* (1898), whose contents include such varied topics as 'Mary's Bonnet', a comic poem about a woman wearing an ostentatious hat in church, 'Nelly o' Bobs', a delightfully cheerful love poem, 'Bite Bigger' and 'A Hawpo'th', reflecting his love of poor children, and many poems on the drudgery, poverty and unemployment experienced by millworkers. Here, for example, is a cry from the heart, the opening lines of a poem based on his own experience of being out of work:

> **Aw've been laikin' for ommost eight wick,**
> **An Aw can't get a day's wark to do!**
> **Aw've trailed abaht t' streets wol Aw'm sick,**
> **An' Aw've worn mi clog-soils ammost throo!**

Sometimes his portrayal of the clog-wearing, poorly-clad, ill-housed worker, wondering where his next meal is coming from, can verge on the sentimental, but his constant touches of dry humour and his stoical optimism made him the most widely read and recited of all the West Riding dialect poets. I still come across old people who learnt John Hartley's poems as children, and still know every word by heart.

The kind of language Hartley used — and to some extent his style and subject matter — is reminiscent of *On Ilkla Mooar*. He even wrote a poem entitled 'Mary Jane', the name of the girl in the song, which starts with a reference to their courting days when they pay a visit to one of his aunts in Bradford:

> **For Mary Jane, Aw'd have yo know,**
> **Had promised me some time ago,**
> **To be mi wife — an' sooa Aw thowt**
> **Aw'd introduce her, as Aw owt.**

The humour of the poem lies in the fact that Mary Jane, though very slim, has a voracious appetite. I am not suggesting that she is in any way connected with the Mary Jane of the song or that John Hartley could have been its author. But reading through his poems, and through the almanacks in general, gives a good idea of the background which produced *On Ilkla Mooar* — Yorkshire dialect as a living language, used to express light-hearted humour, in a homely, unsophisticated way.

Traditional Yorkshire Humour

Closely related to Yorkshire dialect is the style of humour traditionally found in Yorkshire, not unlike that of the North in general, and Lancashire in particular.

One of its best-known characteristics is bluntness. Yorkshire folk tend to say what they mean, to come straight out with an opinion, so that many of their jokes are little more than cheerfully-uttered insults. This may be because historically, hard-bitten Yorkshire farmers and businessmen have so frequently had to bear insults themselves, as in the term 'a Yorkshire bite', usually referring to sharp and cunning Yorkshire dealers, or even 'Tyke', originally from the Viking word for 'bitch', possibly because Yorkshiremen were often seen accompanied by a little terrier. You can see the blunt style in the so-called 'Yorkshire Coat of Arms' *(see page 43)*, where the fly and flea represented sponging and backbiting, the magpie stood for chattering and the gammon of bacon or ham was no good until, like the Yorkshireman, it had been hung up. All this, like the term 'Tyke', was taken in good spirit — the Yorkshireman always been able to laugh at himself, and enjoy the cut and thrust of Yorkshire tit-for-tat wit, a little of which we shall see in the dialogue version of *On Ilkla Mooar* to be considered later.

Another common theme in Yorkshire humour, along with the well-known preoccupation with **brass**, is everything connected with death. I have collected and retold scores of choice anecdotes about death-beds, people filing past open coffins, burials, funeral teas and so forth. Death for those involved is the least funny of all subjects, but humour of this kind has its place in the relief of associated tension. Certainly, it has for a long time been characteristic of Yorkshire people to joke openly — as in the song — about death and burial.

The social conditions have changed, the humour has dated, but the substantial world of late Victorian, chapel-going, hymn-singing working-class Yorkshire can still be glimpsed in the song which, however quaint and quirky it may seem, is nevertheless characteristic of an interesting period of Yorkshire history.

A-Coortin' Mary Jane

We have now considered the two basic components of the song — a popular Methodist hymn tune and the dialect of the West Riding. How did the two come together?

Precisely who the originators of the song were, and where they came from, is still confused and controversial, as we shall see in the next chapter. Much is still mysterious, and has defeated some of the most dedicated investigators. In 1958 a member of the University Song Book Committee stated that in 1922 the committee had tried, and failed, to track down the origin of the song, and that experts like Frank Kidson and Professor F W Moorman had also been baffled by it.

But we can at least clear the ground by looking at the most widely accepted tradition that *On Ilkla Mooar* came into being as a result of an incident that took place during a ramble and picnic on the moor. It is further generally believed that the ramblers were all on a chapel choir outing, from one of the towns in the industrial West Riding.

So let us now take a closer look at the background of the kind of people who are supposed to have first sung the song, mainly in order to see if historical fact makes the tradition feasible.

Life in the Mill Towns

Even if only through William Blake's 'Jerusalem' we know that the green and pleasant land of England was disfigured by 'those dark Satanic mills'. Blake had written this during the Industrial Revolution, the rapid expansion of manufacturing that took place in the late eighteenth and early nineteenth centuries. The earliest date at which I believe *On Ilkla Mooar* could have originated would

Ilkley Moor was a breathing space for Victorian workers from grimy milltowns — in this case Halifax

be around 1850, but more probably some years later. By this time the mills were still dark and soot-blackened, though somewhat less Satanic, because conditions — especially for children — had considerably improved, mainly through reforms introduced by men like Sir Robert Peel, Richard Oastler, Michael Sadler, Lord Ashley and John Fielden.

Even so, life in the Victorian mill towns of Yorkshire was far from pleasant. A typical working week for men consisted of sixty hours — eleven hours a day, with half a day on Saturday. Wages were low, in most cases quite inadequate to support a family. The result was that many women, when not child-bearing, worked full-time (up to ten hours a day) even though they were paid, on average, only half the men's wages, receiving in most cases no more than ten shillings a week. The day began unreasonably early, with the knocker-up man coming round to tap on the bedroom window.

Many workers, still half-asleep, would be in the mill ready for the machinery to start up at 5.30am.

So that the workers would not waste time in walking to work, their houses were often crowded round the mills in long dreary rows. In the first half of the century the population of the West Riding had more than doubled, rising from 564,593 in 1801 to 1,315,885 in 1851. In the second half this trend continued with more and bigger factories and a proportionate increase in minimal housing for the workers. Most lived in conditions we would today regard as intolerable — houses that were small, gas-lit, ill-ventilated, typically built back-to-back, sharing a small yard containing the outside lavatory, described in Yorkshire as a **privy, nessy, petty** or **closit** — all words referring to the tiny private enclosure which was, in fact, a glorified hole in the ground. These smelly earth-closets were the standard form of sanitation until they were gradually replaced by water-closets (most still outside) in the closing years of the century, by which time countless millions of tons of stinking soil-covered excrement had been taken away by the valiant night-soil men.

Sordid, insanitary conditions were found in most of the mill towns, with observers like Engels noting in places like Bradford, Leeds, Huddersfield and Halifax the prevalence of slums where 'the houses are dilapidated and dirty and not fit for human habitation'. He also describes the heaps of refuse in the streets, the choked-up sewers and the generally unhealthy environment of these towns bristling with smoking mill-chimneys. A combination of long hours at work, bad housing, low wages and a poor diet of cheap food (sheep's head boiled with carrots and onions was not uncommon) inevitably led to disease and high mortality, especially amongst young children. People in those days were not cushioned from the stark reality of death as we are today by modern medication and greater life-expectancy. Many died young, and funerals were a prominent feature of social life, until the Public Health Act of 1875 began to make an impact, and the death-rate was gradually reduced.

There was, of course, a brighter side to life in the Victorian mill towns. By no means everybody lived and worked in wretched conditions. Many took a pride in their homes, and even in the poorest areas there was a warm sense of community, with people always ready to help their neighbours. Nor must we forget that the Victorians were great builders, providing splendid town halls, museums, libraries, art galleries, hospitals, churches, chapels — and schools, especially after education was introduced as every child's right by Bradfordian W E Forster's Education Act of 1870.

Moreover, however hard life might have been for the working classes of the industrial towns, there were two great compensations. First, surrounding the grimy huddles of stone-built mills and houses were the wide open spaces of the Pennine hills and moors. Second, within the towns there was available the busy social life based on the churches, and especially the chapels.

Life in the Chapels

Traditionally, the first singers of *On Ilkla Mooar* came from a mill town. Some might have been spinners, weavers, doffers, twisters and turners, familiar with **tops** and **noils**. But not all of them would necessarily be millworkers. Some would have been tradesmen, shopkeepers, clerical workers or housewives, what today we might describe as 'lower middle class'. One thing they all had in common, however, was that they were connected with a chapel, and, in particular, the chapel choir.

Chapels, rather than Anglican or Roman Catholic churches, were the predominant places of worship in Victorian mill towns. The 1851 census of religious attendances showed that in Yorkshire, out of 983,000 who went to a place of worship well over half — 600,000 — went to a chapel or meeting house, and of these the vast majority, 431,000, went to a Methodist chapel. For many people the chapel was the centre of social life, providing companionship, support, entertainment and culture during the week, as well as services on Sunday. It is often forgotten that, long before the 1870 Education Act, chapels no less than Anglican and Catholic churches did pioneering work in elementary education, their Sabbath and Day schools teaching vast numbers of children, not only Christian doctrine in the Sunday school, but reading, writing and arithmetic during the week.

On Sunday, chapel was king. It was not unusual to attend at least three times every Sunday — for the morning service at 10.30 perhaps, for Sunday school or some adult class in the afternoon, and for the evening service at 6.30. The service invariably lasted at least an hour. You entered by the wide-open doors, the steward on duty shaking your hand in welcome. Then you might hang up your cloak or coat in the vestibule, using the protruding wooden or iron pegs which gave rise to that effective Yorkshire description of astonishment, ''**Er eyes stood aht like chapil 'at-pegs!**' You would then find your place in the pew — some pew-places being paid for by a modest rent — and then settle down in a plain but usually lofty building, sometimes with a gallery to increase the seating

A typical Victorian Methodist chapel — Ambler Thorn, Halifax — showing the emphasis on pulpit and the choir.

capacity, and almost always with a full congregation, numbering in the larger town chapels up to 1,000 worshippers.

The service would be very simple in structure — what is sometimes known as the 'hymn sandwich'. There would be a brief call to worship, then the opening hymn, followed by an invocatory prayer — almost always extempore — then would follow Bible readings, a children's address, notices, intercessory prayer and sermon — all sandwiched between appropriate hymns, five in all. The singing would be accompanied and enhanced by music from an imposing organ which rose as an ornate centrepiece behind the pulpit. In front, perhaps on a level with the organist, would be the choir, consisting of a full compliment of sopranos, contraltos, tenors and basses. The chapel choir was highly regarded, not only because it led the hymn-singing, but because it would often perform an anthem, and once or twice a year combined choirs would give an oratorio, such as Handel's *Judas Maccabaeus* or his ever-popular *Messiah*, which many chapel-goers knew by heart.

The service would be led from the pulpit by the minister or, in Methodist chapels, often a local preacher, whose principal contribution was to deliver a sermon. Starting with a text from Scripture, rather than a title, the preacher would expound, illustrate and exhort, going on for the absolute minimum of twenty minutes. In Yorkshire it was customary to pass round at the beginning of the sermon, especially to any children present, what were known as **pew spice**, usually mint imperials or long-lasting humbugs, to be sucked as sweeteners to the sermon.

Sometimes the preacher would be a working man with little formal education, preaching in non-Standard English, and even frank dialect. Colin Dews has written of a Victorian Methodist local preacher from Yeadon called John Preston, a converted poacher and drunkard. Once when he was preaching in Zion Chapel, Holbeck, Leeds, he is reported as leaning over the pulpit and saying:

> **Ah! Me and thee, poor drunkard! Wheeare is-ta? Wheeare is-ta, poor drunkard? Tha mun quit thi way, tha mun indeed,**

or it 'll lead thi dahn. Ah've been i' that rooad missen, an' Ah know summat abaht it ...

Even in my own boyhood I remember Methodist preachers with strong local accents and idioms, and one colourful character who illustrated his sermons with humorous stories in dialect. This raises the question of the extent to which dialect was used by the first singers of *On Ilkla Mooar*. Not all chapel folk — and especially choir members used to singing in Standard English — would speak all the time in dialect. But they would certainly be familiar with it, often making use of it for affectionate humour.

Chapel Courtship and Marriage

Boy-meets-girl was very commonly something that took place in the context of the chapel. Here was an eminently respectable place in which to start courting. Moreover, it was encouraged by chapel-goers in general, pleased to see in the newly-formed attachments the prospect of marriage and children, bringing an increase to the congregation, a guarantee of its future.

Even in my own younger days in the 1940s it was remarkable how the membership of our Methodist chapel was so dependent on intermarriage. Everybody seemed to be at least distantly related to somebody else — so much so that you had to be careful about what you said.

My own courtship of the girl who became my wife was fairly typical. In those days adolescent boys and girls, at least in our chapel, sat separately for the evening service, the girls on the left, the boys on the right, separated by wooden partitions at the end of the central pews. However, with a bit of cunning you could contrive to sit next to the girl of your choice by getting a place at the end of a pew in the centre. I remember the sense of triumph as I sat next to my girl, sharing a hymn book with her, holding it above the wall of partition which separated us.

Though marriages may not always be made in Heaven, they

The way to Ilkley Moor, looking back at Dick Hudson's, with Airedale beyond.

were certainly made in Methodist chapels — and we, forty-five years later, are certainly grateful for the way our romance flourished in a context that some would think of as strict and strait-laced. On the contrary, there was lots of fun in the chapel fellowships, parties and concerts — and on the choir outings. Which brings us to the legendary birth of the song.

Did the first singers come here when the heather was in bloom? One of the author's grandchildren enjoying Ilkley Moor.

A Choir Outing to Ilkley Moor

As we have noted, one of the great compensations for living in a West Riding industrial town was the proximity of open, unspoilt countryside, when those accustomed to drab and dirty surroundings could enjoy the green fields and fresh air. Chapel choirs not only sang together; many of them worked and played together, enjoying each other's company as a group of friends. One of the highlights of the year was the choir outing — a trip to some not-too-distant beauty spot for a ramble, picnic and informal hymn-sing.

The most popular place for such an outing was Ilkley Moor. It was not too far from any of the major towns in the industrial area, yet it was far enough to give a sense of freedom from the workaday world of industrial Yorkshire, with its true but unhappy motto **'Wheeare ther's muck, ther's brass'**.

How did this particular choir party reach Ilkley Moor? The answer obviously depends on which town they came from, but a favourite approach was to go first, by train or wagonette, to Saltaire. Here they would linger a while to admire, perhaps envy, the model village which Sir Titus Salt had built between 1851 and 1871 to show how millworkers really should be housed. Having made his fortune as a pioneer of alpaca wool fabric, he built, as well as his mill on the River Aire, which at one time was the biggest in Europe, a complex of neat houses, complete with schools, hospital, institute and concert hall, and a fine Congregational chapel. With forty-five almshouses and a fourteen acre (5.5ha) park, everything was taken care of — except the needs of drinkers, for Sir Titus, being a teetotal chapel man, would not allow a pub to be built in Saltaire.

After crossing the railway, canal and river, the choir members would now make for Shipley Glen, a pretty wooded ravine just below Baildon Moor. Later walkers (from 1895) would be able to take the Shipley Glen Tramway, but the ascent is not steep. The route now led past Bracken Hall (tea-rooms opened there in 1850) along a boulder-strewn plateau towards Eldwick, soon reaching the famous hostelry known as Dick Hudson's.

Dick Hudson's, the famous hostelry on the edge of Ilkley Moor, as it looked before it was rebuilt on an adjacent site in 1900. Did the words of the song finally take shape in here?

Dick Hudson's is actually the Fleece Inn, dating from 1809. The landlords for three generations were the Hudson family, Richard Hudson or 'Dick' being the publican from 1850 to 1878, when his son John took over, remaining until 1893. The inn was rebuilt in 1900, but is still much the same as in Victorian and Edwardian times, when it was famed for its ham and egg teas, useful as a starting point or stopping place before the hike over the moors, and also as a good place to return to at the end of the day. It is not surprising that the old inn itself has been claimed as the birthplace of the song.

If, as I am assuming, our choir members were typical Methodists, they would not have refreshed themselves at the inn with anything alcoholic. But we can imagine them coming this way and going through the small opening in the wall opposite Dick Hudson's, literally a gateway to the moor, and the walk of nearly four miles

(6.5km) to the Ilkley side. The terrain they covered can have changed very little over the years, gradually climbing over rough grassland until the moor itself is reached — as described on page 14. Those who turned round would enjoy grand views of Airedale, and to the left, a glimpse of the fringe of the industrial area they had left behind, with — if it was later than 1873 — the 250 foot (76m) chimney of Listers Mill in Bradford, big enough, it was said, for a coach and horses to drive round the top.

Just over halfway across the moor, as previously mentioned, they would pass the Twelve Apostles on their right, then soon afterwards begin the descent in Wharfedale, with increasingly glorious vistas unfolding before them. Did they turn right and go directly to the Cow and Calf Rocks? Or did they turn left and go down to White Wells, pause for refreshments, then walk past Ilkley Tarn (where they perhaps saw some ducks) and on to the Cow and Calf? Their final destination could have been Ilkley, where they could have taken a train from 1865 onwards, or they could have walked back to Shipley over the moor via Dick Hudson's, or via Burley and Hollins Hill.

An alternative kind of outing, involving much less walking, could have been a trip by wagonette to the Cow and Calf Rocks — or they could have been picked up there at the end of the day, as envisaged in our cover illustration.

What would they see around them as they walked over Ilkley Moor? Much would depend on the season, of course. A popular time for this ramble was Easter Monday, when there would be little to see of flowers or nesting birds. It could have been in summer, when the heather was in bloom, spreading its lovely purple blanket for miles around, alive with bees and other insects. Whenever it was, there would be the great expanse of sky and breezy moorland, a sense of peace and remoteness. They would fill their lungs with pure fresh air and rejoice in the contrast between all this natural, silent country and the man-made noisy world, enclosed and claustrophobic, which they had left behind for a day, at least.

Such a feeling, as you follow the winding path in the company of friends and fellow choristers, is quite enough to make you want to burst into song. This is where you can let off steam and sing at the top of your voice, without a hint of inhibition. That is how I felt, I remember, in the days of my youth as I walked with a Methodist party over this moor. No prompting would be needed for these choir members to sing. I know from my own experience how they would spontaneously strike up with a favourite hymn, singing in four-part harmony, knowing at least a few of the verses of each hymn by heart.

There is something special about singing hymns under the open sky, particularly if you are a Methodist. The rhythm of the walk and the lungfuls of fresh air seem greatly conducive to it — and there is also this sense of a link with the open-air singing of the early Methodist in the days of the Wesleys ... Whether it was out on the moor or in the shelter of the Cow and Calf, we can be sure that they enjoyed a hearty session of singing.

Two of the choir-members, however, had something other than singing in mind ...

Serenade to a Courting Couple

There is nothing more natural, in a jolly company intent on keeping together, than that a couple interested in each other should want a bit of privacy. So it was with this choir outing. At some point, perhaps after they had stopped for a picnic, one lad — for ever to remain anonymous — slipped away with one of the lasses, whose name was Mary Jane.

Was she an actual person? I see no compelling reason to doubt it. It was common in those days to use two Christian names. Mary, for example, would not have been sufficient by itself if there were other girls called Mary in the choir. In any case, we have seen that John Hartley courted a girl of this name. It is true that in parts of Yorkshire the comment '**sh's a reight Mary Jane**' could mean that the girl was 'a little madam', but this could have been derived from the song.

As far as we know, Mary Jane was the name originally given to the girl, but I have come across one or two alternatives. For example, when *On Ilkla Mooar* was introduced by men from the Penistone district as a 'marching song' for the Sheffield City Battalion in the First World War, one line ran: **'Tha's been a-coortin' our Sar' Ann'**.

Even if the couple were going steady, and their attachment accepted by the rest of the party, they would still want to be on their own. Kissing and cuddling, even embracing and holding hands, was not in those days the sort of thing you did in the presence of others, certainly not in front of your elders and betters in the choir. To make one more reference to my own experience, I know what it is like to go courting on a choir trip ...

The girl who was my future wife became a member of our chapel choir, the prettiest of all the girls in my eyes — and because I was merely a member of the congregation, I could gaze upon her with impunity as she sat up there among the contraltos. Then she invited me to join the annual choir outing. It was a wonderful experience to sing hymns on the coach, but like Mary Jane and her boyfriend, we wanted to be on our own, and when we got to Filey we slipped away from the main party to the seclusion of the sand-hills.

So whether it really happened or not, I find it entirely sociologically and psychologically convincing when it is maintained in the song that these two wandered off over the moor, and equally convincing that when they came back to rejoin the party — perhaps as they assembled at White Wells or the Cow and Calf Rocks — some fellow member of the choir started to pull the leg of the lad who had gone off courting by making up a few lines of dialect verse. It would be just a light-hearted query, a friendly jest, amounting to little more than 'Hello! Now what have *you* been up to?'

His comment might have remained as one of the untold billions of little comments that are uttered, then lost for ever. But it so happened that he found himself singing his question to 'Cranbrook', one of the most popular of the hymn tunes, and one which the choir might just have finished singing.

I do not think that the words were deliberately composed to fit the tune. Whoever originated them simply found himself singing them to the tune that was still running through his head. There is an interesting parallel with another hymn tune used in this way. One of the catchiest of all the Christmas carols is 'O, Come all ye faithful' — so catchy that somebody somewhere, fed up of waiting, suddenly found himself singing to this tune the words 'O, Why are we waiting?' The parallel is even more relevant when we remember that Cranbrook' was also familiar as a Christmas carol when used, particularly in Yorkshire, for 'While shepherds watched'. Indeed, according to Dr Pat Morris and Dr Ian Russell, it was the most commonly-used tune for this carol until 'Winchester Old' was popularised by *Hymns Ancient and Modern* from 1861 onwards.

Once this first wag had struck up with the question in dialect, sung to the tune of 'Cranbrook', we can imagine that other members of the choir would join in — perhaps all of them. There would be no question of learning or rehearsing the words. They are exceptionally simple, even naive, and the refrain is constantly repeated. They have every appearance of something made up on the spot. Later, perhaps, they would have been rounded off over a ham and egg tea back at Dick Hudson's, where it has long been claimed the song actually took shape.

The choir would also join in by contributing other lines themselves — and so would the lad whose leg they were pulling. He even managed to defend himself in quite a spirited way, as we shall see when we now look at what I believe to be the nearest we can approach to the original form of the words.

A Dialogue in Dialect

On Ilkla Mooar was for many years — perhaps for more than half a century — a matter of oral tradition. We have certainly no signed copy of any manuscript or contemporary account of what exactly happened, of who made up the words and when. The nearest approach to anything historical is in the earliest published version of the song — both words and music — which appeared in 1916.

This rarely-seen version, entitled '*On Ilkla Moor baht 'at' – a dialect song from the West Riding*, set to 'Cranbrook', was published in September 1916 as sheet music by J Wood and Sons of Huddersfield jointly with Novello and Co, London. It was collected by Charles H Dennis, a schools inspector who lived at Fartown, Huddersfield. He was something of a composer himself, having written in 1914 the anthem 'Huddersfield: A song of Home' which was sung in the local schools. When published this was described as 'for the boys and girls of Huddersfield' and included evidence of his enthusiasm for Yorkshire in general in his dedicatory letter 'Three cheers for the County of Broad Acres! Old England for Ever!' Dennis was particularly fond of *On Ilkla Mooar*, both words and music, and went round collecting versions 'from those who have sung them — in some cases for very many years'.

The really interesting thing is that this first full record of the oral tradition shows it to have been in the form of a dialogue — comments with responses — setting out what Dennis describes as 'a conversation between a parent and a son'. For all practical purposes this is between a mother and her son, as given below, the women's voices asking the first question, answered in the second verse by the men. Dennis, however, claimed he had heard it sung in some localities with the father as the parent. Here then — with very slight modification in spelling — is the first published version of the song, with my own 'translation' and commentary:

1. Mother **Wheeare wor ta bahn when Aw saw thee,**
(Where were you going when I saw you)
On Ilkla Mooar baht 'at?
(On Ilkley Moor without hat?)

Why this odd reference to the lad being without a hat? Well, in Victorian times everybody wore a hat — and it was immediately noticed that this lad was not wearing his. It is possible that on the windswept moor the lad's hat had been blown away, as our cover illustration suggests. My own view is that he simply left his hat behind with a friend, because he was off for a romp in the heather with Mary Jane. Going courting, even in Victorian times, was hardly a formal activity. Any lad with a modicum of passion and romance would not want to be encumbered with his hat.

The lad, sung by the male voices, now confesses what he has been up to — unlike the commonly-heard version where it is the singers who reveal his secret:

2. Son **Aw wor a-coortin' Mary Jane**
(I was courting Mary Jane)
On Ilkla Mooar baht 'at.

The **Aw** for the first person singular, instead of the usual **Ah**, is significant, and will be commented on later. An interesting variant I have seen is '**Ah wor** *off* **coortin' Mary Jane**'. Could this have been the original? The refrain '**On Ilkla Mooar baht 'at**' is, of course, repeated at the end of each verse.

3. Mother **Aw'll tell thi fatther when 'e comes 'ooame**
(I'll tell your father when he comes home)

The implication is that the son's courtship of this particular girl has not received parental approval — a common enough situation in those days. Or was he a bit wild, always running after the girls, like the lad in the John Hartley poem who '**wouldn't let t' lasses alooane**'? The boy now retorts:

4. Son **Nay, nay, owd lass! Dooan't tak on sooa!**
(No, no, old girl! Don't make such a fuss!)

The verse above is one which Dennis says he has added 'to complete the conversation', but it is a typical comment in authentic dialect.

5. Mother **Tha'll sewerley ketch thi deeath o' cowd**
(You'll surely catch your death of cold)

Whether the hat was blown away, left behind or lost, to have the head exposed to the cold moorland air would be considered by Victorians to be a serious health risk. (NB: Some later versions have **get** or **cop** instead of **ketch**.)

6. Son **Aw'm sewer it wor as wahrm as tooast**
(I'm sure it was as warm as toast)

Were they cuddled together cosily amongst the heather? This, like the next verse, has been added by Dennis.

7. Mother **Tha'll get a bonny month i' bed**
(You'll spend a nice month in bed)

The reference is to a severe chill, and the pneumonia so dreaded by Victorians.

8. Son **Then yo' can come an berry me**
(Then you can come and bury me)

Once again the lad suggests something, rather then having this put to him by the singers, as in most versions.

9. Mother **Then t' wurrums 'll come an eyt thee up**
(Then the worms will come and eat you up)

The idea of worms eating the body of someone who has been buried was far more familiar to people of those days than to us, when burial, rather than cremation, was the standard practice. It could have been suggested by the words that choir members would certainly know from Handel's *Messiah*, quoted from the Book of Job (19:25,26), 'I know that my Redeemer liveth ... And though worms destroy this body, yet in my flesh shall I see God'. References to this text would also be familiar through certain hymns. One by Charles Wesley, not sung today, begins:

I know that my Redeemer lives;
He lives, and on the earth shall stand;
And though to worms my flesh he gives,
My dust lies number'd in his hand.

Another hymn of his includes the lines:

Though the last Judgement Day shall come:
And though the worms this skin devour ...

The pictures of worms may have been reinforced by scriptural references to human beings being little more than worms in the sight of the Almighty (Job 25:6). This image, too, found its way into hymns.

10. Son **Ahr ducks 'll gobble up the wurrums**
(Our ducks'll gobble up the worms)

If the original words were made up on Ilkley Moor, the introduction of ducks might not have been as artificial as first appears. You can still occasionally see ducks on Ilkley Tarn, in those days known as Craig Tarn. Who is to say the first singers did not see some ducks here, foraging for food? The difficulty is that the reference here is to 'our' ducks, though all other versions have '**Then t' ducks...**'.

11. Mother **That feearly maks mi blooid run cowd**
(That really makes my blood run cold)

This is another verse inserted to keep the sequence of responses.

The last three verses given by Dennis, containing material that he has added himself, are exceptional in that they consist of several lines, instead of one with a refrain:

12.
An' yo can gobble up the ducks
An' so get back yer own
An' 'appen they will pizen ye
An' then yo'll keep me company
On Ilkla Mooar baht 'at.

The notion of the ducks poisoning the eaters — though perhaps one of the original jibes — has not survived in any more recent version of the song.

13.
Sooa let us all together gooa
On Ilkla Mooar baht 'at,
Wi Peg an' Kate, John Willie an' Jooa,
Wi Dooad o' Bill's an' ahr Sam Poll,
Wi Ben's lill' lass, an' me an' all,
On Ilkla Mooar baht 'at

Dennis implies that he has added this to show how the singers used to 'improvise verses, some of which contain local or personal allusions'. The names are presumably ones he had heard used in this way, and are all in authentic dialect style, **Dooad o' Bill's** being 'George, son of William' and **ahr Sam Poll** being 'our Sam's Poll' (the possessive typically being dropped) with **Poll** here meaning 'wife' or 'sweetheart'.

14. **O, Ilkla Mooar's booath brooad an' fair,**
Its air so sweet an' fine!
But long the days sin' we ran there:
Aye, long the days sin' we ran there:
The days, the days of Auld Lang Syne!
A cup o' kindness yet,
We'll tak fer Auld Lang Syne.

This last verse is clearly the work of Dennis, with borrowings from Burns. (A version based on this first published form is still available, arranged for two tenors and two basses, from Banks & Son of York.)

How can we reconcile this early dialogue version with the tradition that the words were composed about a courting couple on a choir trip? Well, although there is no reference to a choir, the fact that Dennis found it sung in four parts to 'Cranbrook' fits the story.

Then there is the dialogue itself — exactly the kind of jocular banter we can imagine between one person or group first singing out a challenging remark, then having it answered, each side trying to outdo the other in the style of dry repartee so typical of dialect speakers.

The emphasis in this version is on the parent keeping the son in order, but there is no reason why a choir should not include two generations — indeed, it was not uncommon for children to join their parents to provide continuity. The verse full of names — though we cannot claim they were the original singers — also adds to the idea that this song was made up by a crowd of friends walking over Ilkley Moor.

A Yorkshire Victorian choir outing after their open-air meal. The conductor was moving vigorously, and is therefore blurred.

The four-part and two-part versions Dennis published in dialogue form must already have had equivalents that were a single narrative, still sung in four-part harmony, but with one person, as it were, asking the first question and making all the comments. This is the form, less complicated than the Dennis version, which is mostly now given, as in the sheet provided by the Ilkley Tourist Information Centre. Here it is opposite, with my own slight adjustments of spelling. I see no reason, for example, to write '**oop**' when everybody knows that dialect pronounces 'up' with a broad 'u'; and the second word in the opening should sound like a shortened form of 'was' not 'were'.

1. Wheeare wo' ta bahn when Ah saw thee
   On Ilkla Mooar baht 'at?

2. Tha's been a-coortin' Mary Jane ...

3. Tha's bahn ter get thi deeath o' cowd ...

4. Then wi s'll 'a' ter bury thee ...

5. Then t' wurrums 'll come an' eyt thee up ...

6. Then t' ducks 'll come an' eyt up t' wurrums ...

7. Then wi s'll come an' eyt up t' ducks ...

8. Then wi s'll all 'ave etten thee ...

9. That's wheeare wi get us ooan back!

Claims and Counter-claims

So far we have considered the song as tradition mostly presents it — a leg-pull in dialect, sung to a favourite hymn tune, at the expense of a lad who wandered off with his girl during a choir outing on Ilkley Moor. Although we have no proof that this is anything other than a charming piece of folklore, I maintain that the story is perfectly credible. The fact that the earliest published version was in the form of a dialogue fits in very well with the picture of choir members singing out a line in jest, with other members singing back their response, each trying to outdo the other — the kind of thing that sometimes happens in a jolly gathering.

The Mary Jane in the song need not, of course, have been a member of the choir, but somebody this lad had arranged to meet — possibly even a member of another choir party out on the moor. But because the context suggests she was known to the singers, the most likely explanation is that Mary Jane was one of their number, and that they had realised she had been missing for a while.

There is also the question of where and when the song was put together. The words could have been added to the hymn tune at Dick Hudson's or during the return journey in the wagonette or train — or even at some evening choir rehearsal as they talked about the recent outing. But the sense of immediacy — the reference to the fact that he has been courting Mary Jane, and that he is going to catch his death of cold — suggests something made up during the outing on the moor, or very soon after.

Such possibilities as these are only very slight variables which do not really challenge the traditional account. We must now look at a variety of versions, claims and conjectures which are at odds with what we have so far seen and reconstructed. It is not surprising that when a song has existed as an oral tradition for as long as *On Ilkla Mooar*, there should be all kinds of alternative theories.

A Primitive Version?

It was quite exciting — though ultimately disappointing — to discover that the year before the first published version appeared in 1916, the correspondence columns of a defunct newspaper, the *Yorkshire Weekly Post*, carried words supplied by a Mr A S Robinson of Redcar. Writing in March 1915, he says ' ... enclosed you will find the words of *Ilkler Moor b'aht 'at* as we sang them in Leeds a good many years ago'. His rather primitive version is as follows, notable for the spoken words he adds, to be tagged on to the refrain — something which certain singers still include to this day, though in more varied form.

1. **Ez tha been o' Ilkler Moor?**
   O' Ilkler Moor b'aht 'at.

As in this opening verse, each first line appears three times, with the refrain sung three times.

2. **Tha'll go an' get cowd an' dee ...**
   (*spoken* cos tha went) O' Ilkler Moor b'aht 'at.
3. **An' then we s'all etter bury thee ...**
   (cos tha went) — O' Ilkler Moor ba'ht 'at. etc.
4. **An' then t' worms 'll eyt thee up ...**
5. **An' then t' ducks 'll eyt t' worms ...**
6. **An' then we s'all go an eyt them ducks ...**
7. **Soa then we s'all o' etten thee ...**
   (cos tha went) O' Ilkler Moor ba'ht 'at.

Though interesting, this seems to me a corruption of an earlier version, either because it had gone through mutations in the folk memory, or because this correspondent had misremembered it — or both. I say this because not only is the vital verse about Mary

Jane missing, but because some of the dialect — or the way it is rendered — is incorrect. It is not normal, for example, to reduce 'on' to o' especially before a vowel, as in the awkward **O' Ilkla Moor.** Moreover this same 'o' is used for 'have' in the last verse, which should be **'ave** before a vowel.

In addition, some lines do not scan, and would have been awkward to sing. You can easily see where a missing word or two would give the correct number of syllables if reinstated:

An then t' ducks 'll [come an'] eyt [up] t' worms ...

One verse in this version, however, is surely authentic — and something which C H Dennis unaccountably failed to include in his version — though he did have another line (now usually given as the last or ninth verse) about the singers getting their own back. This last verse in the 1915 version — with better spelling and a word inserted to make it scan — is as follows:

Sooa wi s'll all 'ave etten thee
(So we shall all have eaten you)

This verse, which seems to round off the tale, is now sung as verse eight in most surviving versions.

A Common Alternative

In some of the more recent printed versions we find the following opening verse, which many people always take to be the correct version — mistakenly, I believe, as it was not the version given by the first known collector, C H Dennis:

Wheeare 'es-ta bin sin' Ah saw thee
Where have you been since I saw you
On Ilkla Mooar baht 'at?
On Ilkley Moor without hat?

Contrast this with the 1916 version which is the opening printed for many years in the official guides to Ilkley:

> **Wheeare wor ta bahn when Ah saw thee**
> **On Ilkla Mooar baht 'at?**

Now let us compare these two questions: A. **Wheeare wor ta bahn when Ah saw thee?** B. **Where 'es-ta bin sin' Ah saw thee?** Both could be taken to imply something that had taken place some time before the question was asked, but the statements 'you *have* been courting Mary Jane' and 'you *are going* to get your death of cold' imply that the question was being asked by the singers on the moor — put to the lad after his return from courting Mary Jane.

Both A and B can be made to fit with the addition of 'just now'. A: Where were you off to (just now) when I saw you ... ?' B: Where have you been since I saw you (just now) ... ?' But without this addition B makes it sound — to my ear, at any rate — as though some time has elapsed since the incident. It is almost as if you have just met the man concerned and you ask him 'Where have you been since I saw you (that time) on Ilkley Moor?' — a natural enough question. But if you then say 'You've been courting Mary Jane', it sounds as though he's been doing it since the time you saw him on the moor. Moreover, the next comment would then more logically be: 'I'm surprised you haven't caught your death of cold'.

I am certainly not alone in feeling uneasy about the '**Wheeare 'es-ta bin?**' version. J R Milner of Temple Newsam, for example, writing to the *Dalesman* in 1958, protested that this version missed the point because 'surely the harm was done when the rebuked person was seen on Ilkley Moor, not since'. He adds that the '**Wheeare wor ta bahn?**' version, which he had been taught when young, was always answered by the admission '**Ah wor off cooartin' Mary Jane**'. The '**sin' Ah saw thee**' opening, however, he describes dismissively as one he has heard rendered 'principally by non-Yorkshire men in the army'.

What it boils down to, I suppose, is that both questions make sense if we imagine them being asked there and then on the moor. In that case, though, why is the moor itself referred to? They would hardly have needed to remind the lad where he was. So, whatever was said to him on the moor, it looks as though the song came into being shortly after the event — perhaps on the way home — in which case A (when I saw you) fits better than B (since I saw you).

Another reason for preferring version A is that I think version B could be a corrupted form. To people unfamiliar with dialect, '**bahn**' would be a puzzle. It would therefore be so easy either to mis-hear it or misunderstand it, perhaps deliberately alter it, to '**bin**', as we can see if we juxtapose the lines:

> **Wheeare wor ta bahn ...**
> **Where 'es-ta bin ... .?**

There is, after all, only one vowel in the difference.

You may think there is no point in applying serious textual criticism to such a frivolous song. Who cares which opening line we sing? Well, I do — even if only because sometimes there is a confused beginning when some members of a group sing one opening line and some the other. So in the interest of a harmonious start, as well as keeping to the older tradition, I put in the plea that all Yorkshire folk will strike up with the standard question '**Wheeare wor ta bahn when Ah saw thee?**'

Non-choral Claims

Running counter to the widely-accepted story that the song was made up by members of a choir outing, there are one or two claims that the words were added by some individual. I have, for example, seen the suggestion that it was somebody in a rambling club, or a member of a learned society, who wrote it as a skit on dialect enthusiasts.

My appeals through the press for information produced a number of interesting letters and phone calls from people who had a strong family tradition about '*On Ilkla Mooar*'. For example, Mrs M Bickley, writing from Clayton, Bradford, tells me that her father, born in 1906, had told her that the song was written by a Baildon man. Born in Baildon himself, he had learnt this from his own father, also a Baildon man. In notes to an edition of the song published in 1927 by Beanland and Sons, Ilkley, amongst other possible places of origin Baildon was included, with the chorus **'On Baildon Moor baht 'at'** and the note: 'It is claimed by the Baildoners that the original scene of the courtship which, it was prophesied, was to end in disaster — was on Baildon Moor'. This was confirmed by a Mr L W Tealburton of Leeds, who in 1959 said in a letter to the *Dalesman* that when he was a boy he always used the words 'On Baildon Moor', and called it 'the Guiseley Anthem', the village of Guiseley being not far from Baildon.

Bradford has also been claimed as the place of origin. I have been contacted by a man, who wishes to remain anonymous, who assures me that he once looked after a patient in a Thackley nursing home by the name of Edward Ellis, who claimed that his father, John Ellis, also a Bradford man, had written the words of *On Ilkla Mooar*. He further claimed that as a boy — some time around 1905 — he used to go round selling the song as sheet music in Bradford. The father was apparently killed as a result of a fall down some steps. This version of the origin could be no more than the boy's memory of his father having had the song printed. If it is correct there would have been a printed version before 1916 — but so far I have not been able to find a copy in any of the archives containing ephemera, including the Bradford Reference Library and Local Studies Centre.

One of the most curious claims of all was made in a letter to the Manchester papers by a man from Colne, published in the *Keighley News* of the 1st February 1936. He claimed that the song had been written and sung in Sutton (north-west of Keighley) seventy-three years ago (ie in 1863). His story was that when one of the churches in Sutton ran short of communion wine, a man went to Keighley to buy some. He missed the last train home, so had to walk. Two other men went out from Sutton and met him in Hawkcliffe Wood. 'It was a windy night', says the writer of the letter, 'and his hat had been blown off and lost'. This was, it is alleged, the origin of the song, written by a Sutton man, W Fenegan, the opening lines being:

Wheeare 'ed ta bin when Ah saw thee.
In Hawkcliffe Wood baht 'at?

'This was sung in Sutton as a great joke', added the writer. 'Nothing is said concerning the safe return of the communion wine'.

I regard this story of a Sutton origin as apocryphal. No doubt such words were sung to commemorate an incident which amused the locals — perhaps because somebody got drunk on the communion wine. But the substitution of 'Hawkcliffe Wood' for 'Ilkley Moor' is just one of many we shall consider, and there is no supporting evidence to suggest the Sutton singers were the originators.

There must have been many stories in circulation making a guess at the origin of the song. One of the earliest examples, typical of these vague notions, based on hearsay, appeared in a letter to the *Yorkshire Weekly Post* in January 1915. In this, Thomas Radcliffe of Worksop enquires about a song in which:

> a body is buried, the worms have a feast, then the ducks feast on the worms, then we humans feast on the ducks, the conclusion being that we eat ourselves third-hand.
>
> I am told one line runs 'On Ilkley Moor bar cats', which I cannot make head or tail of. I have seen many Yorkshire ballads, but none with the worm line mentioned. I am also told that at a certain college, male students have adopted the ballad and sing it to a well-known hymn tune.

If we take this last statement seriously, we have to postulate that the dialect verse had come into being before being attached to the hymn tune. But as it does not rhyme, and is, in any case, not impressive as a poem, I cannot really conceive of it having any independent existence.

So we turn from these various claims and speculations to the one that has most supporters — the tradition involving a choir outing. But where did the singers come from?

A Linguistic Clue

One of the most awkward things about the choir-outing theory is that C H Dennis, editor of the first collected version in 1916, makes no mention of it. As far as he is concerned it is:

> a dialect song which, for at least two generations past, has been sung in all parts of the West Riding of Yorkshire and, indeed, wherever the sons of the Riding have foregathered. There is no doubt of the favour it has enjoyed and still enjoys ... for each locality seems to have taken the song to itself.

But although he avoids coming to any decision about the provenance of the dialect, and the home-town of the originators, he gives us, in my view, a clue to the area in the way he spells the first person singular — Aw, instead of the more usual Ah. This is the way the dialect equivalent of 'I' was always spelt in the Halifax area, as we can see in the early editions of the *Clock Almanack* and in both the poems and prose of John Hartley, including, for example, the appropriate lines:

> **Coortin' days, coortin' days — loved one and lover!**
> **What wod Aw give if those days could come ovver!**

Having grown up in Wibsey, close to Halifax, I am especially familiar with the dialect of that area, and am convinced that I hear it in the words of *On Ilkla Mooar*. Not that this amounts to proof, but at least it lends support to the popular view that the song has its roots in the Halifax district.

The Claims of Halifax

Outings to Ilkley Moor came from all the towns of the industrial West Riding, but tradition favours Halifax, or somewhere close to it, as the place from which the legendary choir outing came. This was certainly the view of Halifax researchers such as Eve Chapman.

Alleged points of origin within the town are various ... Was it the sturdy, square building of the Providence Congregational Chapel

Providence Congregational Chapel, Ovenden, built in 1837. Did the choir outing come from here?

at Ovenden, built in 1837? This is maintained by Jack Waring, formerly of the *Halifax Courier*, with even the hint that the first singing of the song might have taken place in the green fields just off the road further down, Ovenden Flat, once a favourite spot for picnics. Support for this comes from an early variant of the chorus:

On Ovenden Flat baht 'at!

Although this adds a slightly awkward extra syllable, it has a rhyme — something of which the standard version of *'On Ilkla Mooar'* is devoid. This refrain was certainly sung, but presumably, like later versions we shall consider, because it was substituted by the locals for the original.

Another strong contender is one of the Halifax Methodist chapels — Ebenezer Primitive Methodist, first built in 1822. The name 'Primitive' should not be taken to indicate anything uncouth. This term described a movement founded in 1811 intended to recapture the evangelistic fervour of early Methodism, as distinct from the more formal Wesleyan Methodists. Though Congregationalists may well have been the first to put words to the hymn tune, it is perhaps more likely to have been Methodists, especially Primitive Methodists, long noted for their rousing open-air singing.

References to the presumed outing from Halifax to Ilkley Moor sometimes use the term 'church'. We see this in an account by G E Fox in the British Council magazine *Britain Today* (1952) which makes the statement: 'Round about 1886 a Halifax church choir went to picnic on Ilkley Moor'. Here the term 'church' can mean Anglican churches, for example, as well as chapels. This ambiguity may have favoured the assumption that the choir was indeed a Church of England one. At least one person, who happens to be the father of the conductor of the Filey Fishermen's Choir, has always maintained that the original singers were the choir of Halifax Parish Church.

Ebenezer Primitive Methodist Chapel (1822) — another Halifax chapel from where the first singers could have come.

The Heptonstall Glee Choir

What at first sight is a challenge to the Halifax theory is the statement made by Wallace Harvey of Whitstable, Kent, that when he was researching the life of Thomas Clark of Canterbury, he was told that it was the Heptonstall Glee Choir who in 1877 took Clark's tune, 'fitting to it the words of *On Ilkley Moor baht 'at*'. He first stated this in a short account he wrote in 1959, adding in his fuller published account of 1983 that it was the conductor of the glee choir who composed the words, and that he had been told this by 'an old Yorkshire schoolmaster'. In discussing this with Wallace Harvey, I have further learnt that this was Frank Newsome, headmaster of a boy's school at Whitstable from 1935 to 1960. He had told him that the choir went round by wagonette, giving concerts in the district. Such glee clubs usually consisted of men only, but wives and sweethearts could have accompanied the annual outing.

Is this something approaching definitive historical evidence concerning the origin? The difficulty is that so far I have not been able to find any record of a glee choir in Heptonstall, though with a population of over 3,000 in 1877 the township would easily have been able to support one. It was then a somewhat remote community in the Pennines, famous for its Octagon Methodist Chapel, built in 1764 by John Wesley (today the oldest chapel of its kind in continuous use). Heptonstall, though about eight miles (13km) to the west of Halifax, was linked to it in a friendly rivalry, as is shown by the old dialect saying:

> **Halifax is built o' wax,**
> **Heptonstall o' stooan:**
> **I' Halifax ther's bonny lasses,**
> **I' Heptonstall ther's nooan.**

If the Heptonstall claim is true, then at least we are still within the Halifax area, and a way of reconciling these two main traditions is that the glee choir may simply have been the first to sing *'On Ilkla Mooar'* in public, without necessarily being the originators.

An Ilkley Origin?

The fact that the name of Ilkley is in the title and the refrain has led some to assume that the song was composed by an inhabitant of this town. I have seen it stated in recent years that Amy Taylor, an Ilkley dressmaker, 'made up the tune when at work'. This must be derived from the claim made by G E Fox in 1952:

> An old lady, who still lives in Ilkley, heard the song the day after it was born. It was sung by a young woman called Amy Taylor, one of the choir who had invented it, as she sewed at her table in the little dressmaker's shop where she worked.

The name of Amy Taylor, then, is the only one to have come down to us of a person present, as a choir member, when the words were added to the hymn tune. What is not clear is where she came from and where she worked. The informant, we are told, was still living in Ilkley (in 1952). But this does not necessarily mean that Amy Taylor was herself an Ilkley person. All we are told is that she was a member of 'the choir' which, in the previous paragraph of this same account is said to have come from Halifax.

The Problem of Chronology

You will have noticed that we already have a problem with the date of when the song was first sung. The Halifax tradition is that the visit is supposed to have been in 1886, the Heptonstall claim is 1877. Neither of these dates is supported by documentary evidence, and both of them seem rather late. Let us look at some of the estimates that have been given of when *'On Ilkla Mooar'* first appeared.

Some, as we might expect, are little more than guesses, the feeling that the song is very old. In our boyhood, my pal and I used to try out the various routes in *Yorkshire Walks from Bradford* by 'Wanderer' (Eric Lodge), which first appeared in 1938. In the walk entitled 'Baht 'at ower Ilkla Mooar', the author refers to 'yond breezy uplands that gave birth to Yorkshire's National Anthem ... a parody anonymously composed in Bradford over a century ago'. His assumption that the song was of Bradford origin may be as wide of the mark as his guess at the date. A full century earlier would have given us 1838 — far too close to the time when the hymn was just becoming established, I would have thought. The irreverent misuse of a sacred melody would not have been acceptable so early in the Victorian era. Even by 1860, if it already existed, it was not sufficiently known (or regarded) to be included in Ingledew's *Ballads and Songs of Yorkshire*, published that year.

Some have suggested that the song was not heard much before the First World War, but there is clear evidence that it was being performed in public in about 1897, when a Mr R Drake, remembered hearing it sung by a travelling concert party in the Old Town Hall, Scarborough. We can push it much further back than this, though. As already mentioned, C H Dennis, writing in 1916, spoke of the song being sung 'for at least two generations past'. If we take the *Oxford English Dictionary* definition of a generation — 'about 30 years' — this means that going back sixty years from 1916, we arrive at 1856 — earlier, if we accept the 'at least' two generations.

This earlier date of origin is nicely confirmed, I think, if we accept a statement made by the anonymous writer of notes issued with the Beanlands edition of the song published in February 1927:

> ... the ditty has been a treasured possession of the West Riding people for at least forty to fifty years before its publication in 1916. The present writer — a comer-in — was introduced to *Ilkla Mooar* in the latter part of 1879, and several of his contemporaries among his Yorkshire friends have told him that they, now sexagenarians and septuagenarians, have sung it from their youth up, even from their childhood days.

Though I do not normally find figures of this kind interesting, the arithmetic here provides a little detective work and leads us to the conclusion that if we take one of these friends aged seventy in 1927 back to his childhood days, say to the age of ten, we arrive at 1867.

This is a more accurate calculation than the one which assumes a generation to be thirty years. We can be more confident about the Dennis figure of 1856 and the Beanlands figure of 1867, concluding that *On Ilkla Mooar baht 'at* could well have originated in the early years of the second half of the century, and not as late as 1877 or 1886, the dates quoted for Heptonstall and Halifax respectively.

Ringing the Changes

There is a kind of poetic justice in the fact that a song which is entirely an adaptation of something else should itself have been adapted. We are now so accustomed to the refrain '**On Ilkla Mooar baht 'at**' that it is surprising to learn that this was only one of many versions. If each version were to be taken seriously, then the whole business of the hatless lad courting Mary Jane could have taken place — according to the variants I have so far found — at no fewer than twelve different locations, in addition to Ilkley.

Does this mean, then, that Ilkley Moor was not necessarily where the song was originally set? Well, though that remains possible I can only say that because the other places sung about are so numerous — rather than just one or two well-attested rivals — it is far more likely that over the years people who sang the song, perhaps on returning from a trip to Ilkley Moor, substituted the name of a moor or picnic spot near their home town. The variation in place probably amounted to little more than other variations in the text and the spoken or shouted comments which it became the custom to add — all part of the spontaneous nature of the song.

Here, then, are the alternative versions, with the location identified. We will start with those in Halifax and Calderdale, another bit of support for the tradition that this is where the choir first came from:

1 On Ovenden Flat baht 'at!

As already mentioned this is a picnic area, once visited by wagonettes, situated between Lee Bank Cross and Ovenden Top, not far from Providence Chapel.

One of the rocks near the Cow and Calf inscribed with Victorian graffiti, in this case from Sowerby Bridge in 1875.

2 At Sarby Brig baht 'at!

Sowerby Bridge is south-west of Halifax, closely adjoining it. This shortened form of its name was popularised by the song '**Ah come fra Sarby Brig**' sung by a dialect comedian Tom Foy, whose dry humour still survives on scratchy 78s made in the early 1900s. Sowerby Bridge, incidentally, is one of the place-names carved by Victorian visitors into the Cow and Calf Rocks.

3 At Luddenden Fooit baht booit!

This has a nice comic ring to it, provided it is pronounced in correct dialect style, with the separation of the vowels — '**foo-it**' and '**boo-it**' (boot). Luddenden Foot is also close to Halifax, situated a mile or so up the Calder from Sowerby Bridge.

4 I' Saltrubble Docks baht socks

This strange-looking location is near Halifax and is, in fact, Salter Hebble, a picturesque point on the canal between Halifax and Elland.

5 On Lindley Mooar baht 'at

We now move to the Huddersfield area, Lindley Moor being situated about two miles (3km) to the north of the town. Though now crossed by the busy M62 (between junctions 23 and 24), this was once a well-known green space ideally suited to the recreational needs of the workers in the nearby industrial community. In 1897 about sixteen acres (6.5ha) of land there, including Wappy Rocks, had been bought for £510 by Councillor T H Moore, who had sold them to Huddersfield Council for the use of the public. This part of Lindley Moor, said a press report, with its magnificent views over the Stainland and Halifax valleys, stretching from Blackstone Edge to Queensbury, was 'visited by many inhabitants of the borough'. It was a popular outing by tram, as Huddersfield had run trams there since 1873 — the first municipal tramway in the British Isles.

6 Dahn Ahtloine Flat baht 'at

This is the local way of saying 'Down Outlane Flat, without hat' — like the Ovenden Flat version, providing a rhyme. Outlane Flat is part of the Lindley Moor green space, about a mile (1.5km) to the west of junction 23 of the M62.

Two clear references to Huddersfield could make it a rival of Halifax as the provenance of the song. Indeed, I have been told by Mrs Hilda Thornber of Elland (situated between Halifax and Huddersfield) that she had always understood *On Ilkla Mooar* to have originated in Huddersfield, where it was made up by a chapel choir and 'sung as a round'. This reference to the way it was sung certainly fits in with the dialogue version given by C H Dennis, but the fact is that though Dennis collected the song while living in the town, he made no claim that Huddersfield was the place of origin. If any claims and counter-claims arise between Halifax and Huddersfield, we have to set this in the context of the friendly rivalry that has long existed between these two towns separated by only a few miles.

7 On Emley Moor baht 'at

We now move to the east of Huddersfield to a high moorland area easily reached by people living in textile and mining towns like Dewsbury, Wakefield and Barnsley, the Emley Moor now crowned by the well-known landmark of the television mast.

8 Dahn Ee Mooar Loine baht 'at!

This less common variant, 'Down High Moor Lane', refers to a location near the village of Clifton, Brighouse. So we are still not far from Halifax.

9 In Hawkcliffe Wood baht 'at!

This is the version from Sutton, near Keighley, already referred to.

10 On Baildon Mooar baht 'at!

This, again has already been noted.

11 On Mottram Mooar baht 'at

Watch out! We have now strayed over the border into Lancashire. Mottram Moor is just south of Stalybridge. Even deeper into foreign territory, to the north-west of Stalybridge, we have a version associated with Oldham:

12 On Owdham Edge baht 'at

This is of particular interest because it was the chorus of a version of the song adopted by soldiers from the Oldham area in the first World War. In this history of the 42nd (East Lancashire) Division, published just after the war in 1920, F P Gibbon comments:

Each brigade or unit had its favourite songs and its own peculiar jokes, many of which were incomprehensible to the outsider. Perhaps none was quite so esoteric as the weird lament of the 10th Manchesters, known in three continents and many countries as *On Owdham Edge beaut 'at* (sung to an old Methodist tune combining swing and solemnity), wherein the gruesome fate of the lad who, without head-covering, courts Mary Jane upon that eminence is foreseen by the fond parent ... First a cold, then death, burial, eaten by worms, worms devoured by ducks, which in turn appear upon the family dinner-table. 'Then we's soon be ettin' thee', begins the last verse of this lugubrious but fascinating lyric.

There is no suggestion here — let it be carefully noted — that the song could have originated in Oldham, on **t' wrong side o' t' Pennines** as dialect speakers sometimes teasingly refer to Lancashire. It is simply that this regiment, raised in the Oldham area, borrowed the Yorkshire song and made it their own.

Tempting though it is to find another setting for Mary Jane and her unknown admirer, the great majority of versions — even some which have changed the place name in just some of the verses — have always set the scene on Ilkley Moor.

The Murder of Mary Jane — and other Strange Tales

When the origin of a curious song is lost in the mists of mythology, it is only to be expected that a number of speculative theories will be produced, with the inevitability of air rushing in to fill a vacuum. But what hit the headlines in June 1986 was not another theory, but something purporting to be a hard piece of documentary evidence.

The Skeleton on the Moor

Yorkshire eyes must have stuck out like proverbial **chapel 'at pegs** on the morning of the 13th June 1986 when they saw in the *Yorkshire Post* the headline:

'Skeleton on Moor' clue to origins of song

This introduced a short news-story given to the press by Mary Sara, secretary of the Ilkley and District Arts Federation. She claimed that she had received 'a mysterious but apparently authentic letter' from an eighty-six year old woman, Vera Hainsworth, who had written to the federation from Birmingham. The contents of the letter were sufficient for the *Yorkshire Post* to speak of 'discoveries about the origin of the song "On Ilkla Mooar baht 'at" which indicate that the Mary Jane it refers to could have been a murder victim'. The headline in the *Ilkley Gazette* on the same day was even more dramatic:

Was Mary Jane buried on Ilkley Moor?

Whereas the *Yorkshire Post* gave a brief summary of the claim made in the letter from Birmingham, the *Ilkley Gazette* quoted it in full. It begins:

> I am as old as this century, and left Ilkley with my husband after the First World War to move south. My Uncle Ernest, who must have been about sixty at the time, took me on one side the Christmas before my husband and I were due to leave Ilkley. He swore me to secrecy and told me the following tale.

Unfortunately no dates are given, but if this Christmas was soon after the war, say in the 1920s, and her uncle was 'about sixty', his teenage years, which he went on to mention, must have been at least forty years further back, giving us some time before 1880 as the date of this discovery. The letter continues:

> That Christmas we had a sing-song around my mother's piano, including a rendering of *On Ilkley Moor*. My uncle asked me if I knew the origin of the song, and I had to admit I didn't.
>
> He then explained to me that a group of his friends had got together in their late teens and formed an archaeological society. They were primarily interested in Roman remains and did a lot of digging round the parish church area and, indeed, discovered a couple of coins there.
>
> Their interest had led them to do some excavating on the moors by the Druid Stone. In their digging by a cup and ring stone a few hundred yards away from the Druid Stone they unearthed a skeleton, which initially they thought must have been Iron Age, until they discovered an emerald locket with the inscription 'To MJP 1825, with love'.

The general background given here is plausible. The Ilkley area has long been a favourite place for archaeological digs. We are left wondering, though, why these young men started digging in this particular area.

Realising that the discovery of this valuable locket in such an unlikely situation might take some believing, the letter writer adds that she can vouch for the truth about the locket, as her uncle gave it to her, and she had it in her possession 'until the 1950s'.

We now come to the passage that emphasises the macabre atmosphere associated with burial in a remote part of the moor, as is reflected in the song. There is even a hint of one of the ducks that has eaten eaten up the worms:

> On top of the human remains was a skeleton of a large bird. My uncle and his friends, so he says, were scared stiff by their discovery, and swore each other to secrecy.

This is followed by the revelation we have all been waiting for — the point of origin of the song, with the name of the author:

> Uncle Ernest's friend, Jim Smith, who often visited us in Ilkley, lived over in the Calderdale area, and was in the local choir. Uncle Ernest told me that he'd written a song with a few choruses based on their discovery on the moor ... Was the 'MJP' on the locket the Mary Jane of the song, and was the bird the goose?

Why the letter refers to a goose rather than a duck is a mystery, not fitting with any known version of the song. The last paragraph of the letter seems to suggest that the secret has been kept for so long because those who knew were too frightened to speak of it:

> I do know that Uncle Ernest always kept away from the moors, and had great fear even when as a girl I used to walk up to White Wells to take the waters.

So now we know. It was Mary Jane, not her hatless lover, who ended up being buried on the moor. And it was Jim Smith, inspired by the story of the gruesome discovery, who wrote a song which, unaccountably, got it all wrong.

Don't believe all you read in the newspapers! This was manifestly a hoax, though reasonably subtle. It was a nice touch to have 'Jim Smith' located in Calderdale — the Halifax area — and as a member of the choir.

Nor can we dismiss the idea of murder on the moor as having some possible connection with the song. One tradition from the Shipley area is that the story about burial on the moor owes its origin to the murder of a rent collector that took place in Nab Wood in November 1839. Another Ilkley murder of more relevant date took place in July 1856, when a body was found at the bottom of a ravine near Cowpastures by a woman staying at the Hydropathic Establishment at Ben Rhydding.

Two linguistic slips, however, betray the forger of the letter. Neither an eighty-six year old lady nor her uncle would, I believe, have used the word 'initially' instead of 'at first' — a comparatively recent fashion. Then the letter uses the phrase 'so he says' of the uncle who has been dead for many years.

It is no coincidence that this letter was released to the press shortly before the Ilkley and District Arts Federation staged a midsummer musical at the Cow and Calf Rocks to celebrate the centenary of the song, presumed to have been written (though probably wide of the mark) in 1886. I have spoken to Keith Hartley, who, at the time of the publication of the letter in 1986, was chairman of the federation. I put it to him that it was a clever publicity stunt. He assured me that he had definitely seen the letter, written 'in shaky handwriting', but he had no idea what had happened to this crucial document. 'Yes', he finally conceded, 'it could have been a hoax — but it makes a good story, doesn't it?'

A Sensational Literary Discovery

What if the dialect poem was just a light-hearted version of a serious original in Standard English?

In the October 1925 issue of the *Highway*, a journal associated with the Workers' Educational Association, there appeared an article headed 'Ilkley Moor — A Literary Discovery'.

Here was something even more eye-opening than the discovery of a skeleton — the original poem on which the dialect doggerel was based. In his introduction, the editor described *On Ilkla Mooar* as 'a catch or glee commonly sung by students at WEA summer schools, and sometimes called "The Yorkshire Anthem"'. This had recently been traced, he claimed, to its proper literary source by one of the tutors who had recited his discovery at Oxford. The tutor is not identified, except by the initials B I M at the end of the poem. The editor continues, 'It appears that the present anthem is really a debased dialect version of a poem which the internal evidence of its style enables us to attribute it to Longfellow'.

The editor first sets out a version of the dialect song, interesting in itself as it includes a change of tense — 'had', rather than 'has' — and is more like Standard English. Under the title he has already mentioned, 'The Yorkshire Anthem', it begins:

Where had ta bin sin' I saw thee
On Ilkley Moor baht 'at?
Tha'd been a-courtin' Mary Jane ...
Tha's baun' to get th' death o' cowld ...

Then, under the name 'H W Longfellow', he sets out a long poem in blank, convoluted verse in a style reminiscent of *Hiawatha* and other Longfellow poems:

This is the moorland primeval, the far-famed moorland of Ilkley
Where the breezes blow in the bracken, and yellow and
prickly the gorse grows;
Twixt the valley of Wharfe and the river that runneth from
Skipton ...

We are now introduced to John Smith of Ilkley. One autumn evening he has wandered away over the moor, leaving behind his friends who are still in the town enjoying a drink in the bar of the Blue Boar, joking and singing in dialect:

Mirthful were they with song and the fearsome speech of their
county

John is walking over the moor 'in amorous rapture' with his sweetheart, her identity, with brief biographical details, now being revealed:

Leaning her hand on his arm, went a maiden modest and
buxom,
Mary her name was, and Jane, a not unknown combination;

Fifteen years had she grown in the distant township of Pudsey,
Fifteen years had she cooked in the house of Tompkins the
brewer ...

This presumably means that she had lived in Pudsey and worked as a cook for that length of time, not that she was only fifteen. Indeed, her description now shows Mary Jane to have been a mature woman, to say the least:

Fifteen stone was her weight on the scale at the gate of the
goods-yard
And of a girth proportioned, her waist the despair of her lover.

Now we come to the origin of the 'baht 'at' refrain in the lengthier Longfellow original:

Happy was he in his love. But, alas for the rashness of lovers,
He had departed in haste from the home where he dwelt with
his mother,
Hasting away from her side to his love and the place of her
trysting,
Leaving his tea untouched, and his hat on the hatpeg maternal,
Hatless he went in the breeze, the treacherous breeze of the
autumn;
Chilly it blew on his brow and the place where the tresses had
once been;
Till ere the evening closed a piteous catarrh was upon him,
Chilled was he through to the brain, and hampered his
utterance ecstatic.
Never was warmth in the heart a cure for a cold in the cranium.
So ere the day came again for the tryst and the walk with his
lover,
Lonely was she on the earth, and hatless was he in the churchyard.

John Smith, we are now told, lay in his grave, on the edge of the moor, while his spirit went to knock in vain at the gates 'where never a Yorkshireman enters'. It is what happened to his body, however, that interests the poet. In his lines on the seething hordes of worms eating up the mortal remains of Smith, he spares us nothing:

> When from the north and the south, from the region of dawn and of sunset,
> Gathered a mighty assemblage, an army of countless battalions,
> Scenting the banquet afar, the myriad lords of the subsoil.
> Feasted they there through the night, and feasted they there through the morrow;
> Some made repast of the feet that had trodden the paths of the moorland,
> Some of the arms that had clasped, and the heart that had beat for his Mary,
> Some of the hatless head, and the brain, a meagre refection.
> So was the feasting ended; and up to the air of the moorland,
> Piercing their way through the sod, to the pattering call of a rainstorm,
> Up to the air and the grass departed the revellers sepulchral.
> With them passed from the grave, in a thousand organs digestive,
> Back to the moor that he loved, the mortal remains of the lover.

Next comes the spoof original of the line about the ducks coming along to eat up the worms. The beginning of this is somewhat confusing, because of the back-to-front word order sometimes found in Longfellow. The 'they' in the first line refers to the worms:

> But when they came to the air and the grass of the churchyard,
> Seeking their food in the mud and splashing about in the puddles
> Met them the agents of fate relentless, three ducks and a duckling.
> Then was there heard on the moor the sound of a gobbling prodigious;
> This way and that in their greed and their glee went the ducks and the duckling,
> Gobbling to right and to left; and never they ceased from their gobbling.

The closing lines of the poem make the most of the laconic '**then wi s'll all 'ave etten thee**'. The scene is back in the Blue Bull, where John Smith's friends are enjoying a splendid meal in honour of their deceased friend:

> Feasted the friends of Smith, and loud was the noise of their feasting,
> Save when in solemn silence they drank to the dear departed.
> Little they recked as they ate of the flesh of the ducks and the duckling,
> How it was formed, and where, of the succulent substance of earth-worms,
> Nor where the worms had found their source of delectable juices.
> So by devious ways and a transmigration of bodies,
> Hatless e'en as he went, John Smith had returned to his cronies.

This literary hoax, even more than the archaeological hoax, is of interest because it testifies to the popularity of *On Ilkla Mooar* in the 1920s, well beyond the boundaries of Yorkshire, and especially amongst students. By the beginning of the twentieth century it had already become a reference point, a unique kind of folk song enjoyed for its rare combination of dialect and dark humour.

A Source of Modern Irony

On Ilkla Mooar is so well known that it is easy to make it the butt of modern satirical humour and weave all kinds of silly stories round it — just for fun, like the first compilers of the song. In June 1988, for example, a *Dalesman* article, signed 'W', spoke amusingly about the song, offering an explanation of the chief motivation for writing it. 'Whom would the verse benefit?' asks the writer. 'The reiteration of hatlessness associated with death points decisively to the hatters.' Fearing that a fashion for not wearing hats might take over, the local vendors of headgear had made a collective effort in the song to warn those who go hatless to beware of the fatal conseq-uences.

This tongue-in-cheek humour was then taken up by R Hindley, who wrote in mock-solemn style of the archaeological and anthropological aspects of the song:

> ... it is sufficiently clear from the terse language of the lyric that it seeks to transmit the ancient and traditional interpretation of the Mesolithic and Bronze Age funerary monuments which characterise the moor, and the demise of those occupants is imaginatively (yet credibly) attributed to the climatic hazards of the habitat together with the absolute need for protective clothing.

The writer now advances his own lunatic theory. The song was written to draw attention to the cup and ring markings which are a conspicuous feature of the moor:

> R W B Morris has enumerated 104 different explanations of these enigmatic symbols, but our anonymous author (of the song), doubtless guided by folk memory, has added a 105th — namely, that the rings represent worms and the cups are peck-marks of ducks.

To this nonsense he adds in all seriousness a footnote admitting that Morris did liken the carvings to copies of worm casts, but he 'failed to establish the crucial linkage to the worm which in much early myth encircles the earth and symbolises eternity by its evident lack of beginning or end'.

An Eye-witness Account

The best satirical piece I have come across concerning *On Ilkla Mooar* appeared in *Yorkshire Life* in August 1974. In this George Marvill relates what he claims to be the true story behind the song: 'What follows is (so help me God) a true and unvarnished statement of all that is known'. He even gives us a precise date, rather cleverly, in winter. On Saturday the 18th December 1905, he tells us, members of the Eckerslyke Wesleyan chapel choir set off on their annual walk over the moor to Ilkley. They were led by their organist and choirmaster, Jonas Umpleby, who was a disquieted man, partly because of the unruly behaviour of his principal tenor, Handel Hardaker, who liked his pint of ale and often went around '**baht 'at**', a symbol of depravity, and partly because of the attachment of Jonas's daughter, Mary Jane, to Willie Beevers, 'his far-from-principal baritone', a lad who seemed to him to have no future.

Eventually the choir arrived at the Cow and Calf Rocks, the ideal place for the singing of carols in the open air. It was noticed that three of the choir members were now missing — Handel Hardaker, who was assumed to have nipped off for a drink, and Willie Beevers with his sweetheart Mary Jane:

> 'Ah s'll ha' summat ter say to 'er abaht this', said Jonas Umpleby crossly to his wife. Then, to the choir: 'Well, dooan't stand abaht gassin', else it 'll bi dark afooare wi mek a start. Ger aht yer "Angels from the Realms o' Glory". Watch my beat, an' sing it *feelin'ly*.'

Now they were rejoined by Handel Hardaker, in particularly good voice, and went on to sing 'While Shepherds Watched' to the tune 'Cranbrook'. They sang the first verse, and were about to burst into the second, when they were halted by a ribald peal of laughter from Handel Hardaker. They all turned and saw Mary Jane, arm-in-arm with Willie Beevers, coming down from the moor. When they had last seen him Willie was wearing a billy-cock hat, but now 'his ruffled locks were exposed to the crisp December air'.

> Jones let out an angry bellow. 'Wheeare 'as-ta been?' he bawled. 'E's been a-coortin' Mary Jane,' tittered Ezra Hardcastle (tenor). 'Willie Beevers!' screamed Willie's Aunt Maggie (soprano). Whativver art-ta thinkin' on, walkin' abaht on Ilkla Mooar baht 'at? Tha's bahn ter catch thi deeath o' cowd!'

Then it was, in the mercurial mind of Handel Hardaker, rendered yet more nimble by pints of Emmersley ale, that six iambic syllables began to pulsate ... 'While shep-' ... 'Wheeare 'as-ta bin ... ' He could bear it no longer. He burst instantly into song. The tune was 'Cranbrook': the words, alas, were not those of the Christmas hymn.

Thus the song came into being, George Marvill assures us, in 1905, exactly 100 years after the tune was composed!

It was infectious. After the first line, one or two choir members joined in, then half a dozen, then everybody, except Mr and Mrs Jonas Umpleby and Willie Beevers's Aunt Maggie:

Willie and Mary Jane, both blushing now, arrived to the sound of the choir singing in full-throated harmony:

Tha's been a-coortin' Mary Jane
On Ilkla Mooar baht 'at! (baht 'at!)

A mist, tantalising and impenetrable, shrouds for ever the subsequent history of the people in the story. Did Willie Beevers marry Mary Jane? We don't know. By what happy accident did he appear on the scene (baht 'at) at that propitious moment? One likes to think that his hat tumbled from his head during the course of a long and passionate embrace. But nobody really knows.

Exactly. Because nobody really knows, we are at liberty to imagine whatever we like. And this playful reconstruction may not be too far from the truth. Many a true word is spoken in jest.

Fun with Baht 'at

This is the best-known phrase in the song, especially it is often the custom to echo it after the refrain, either by shouting it or, better still, by the basses singing it. Incidentally, you won't find **baht** in an ordinary dictionary — except as the name of the standard monetary unit in Thailand.

There is no doubt whatever that **baht 'at** simply means 'without hat' or, if you like, 'without a hat'. This, as we have seen, is the obvious reason for the suggestion that the lad in the story is going to get his death of cold and die. However, alternative explanations have been given, and deserve to be briefly examined.

The first is the suggestion that '**baht 'at**' may be a corruption of something like 'be (I) 'at'. Victor Brooks of Brighouse assures me that his mother, born in Rastrick at the end of the last century, always said that it was originally a phrase like this, used to mean 'On Ilkla Mooar — that's where!' The use of **baht** for 'without', however, is very well-established. In parts of the West Riding it is still used in phrases like '**Ah'm baht brass**', sometimes shortened to '**Ah'm baht**', meaning 'I've no money on me'. The phrase **suppin' baht** can also be used, apparently, by pub drinkers when it is somebody else's round.

Several dialect jokes testify to how commonly **baht** was once used. For example, there is the story of the West Riding lad in the army who had turned up on parade without a rifle. On being asked by the officer for an explanation, he replied '**Ah 'a'n't got nooan**'. The officer asked the next soldier what on earth this meant, only to receive the reply '**E says 'e's baht**'. Then there were the two little lads looking up at a well-known statue which had the inscription 'Sir Titus Salt, Bart' (ie baronet). One of them asked, '**What does 'bart' mean?**' The other looked up at the statue and said '**Baht 'at, o' course!**'

The most far-fetched explanation about the original meaning of **baht 'at** appeared in the correspondence column of a national paper in 1959, when somebody from Twickenham wrote:

> The '**at** is not 'hat', but the local pronunciation of '**owt**', which means 'anything'. In other words, the chap concerned was on Ilkley Moor without his clothes. That explains why the saying goes on to say that he would catch his death of cold.

The editor added the comment: 'What? He went courting Mary Jane *naked*, sir? Come, come, come!'

This explanation has a certain comic appeal, but can be dismissed as nonsense. Quite apart from it being extremely unlikely that the two words would be confused by dialect speakers, it is far too fanciful to imagine that easily-shocked Victorian hymn singers would celebrate nudity in this way. The implied attitude to sexual matters — both the lad being stark naked and somebody singing about it — is far more typical of modern times. No. The proprieties of the period mean that the exposure was no more than that of a young man who had been courting, fully clothed, except for his hat.

Yet another explanation of the origin of **baht 'at** — this time patently facetious — appeared in the pub-guide pages of *Pennine Magazine* in August 1982. Here we are told of a bowlderised reference to the 'tap' or 'tap room' (public bar) of the Ilkley Moor pub, the original line of the song having been:

In t' Ilkla Mooar Bar tap

Oddest of all is the assumption I referred to at the beginning of the book that **baht 'at** is a place on the moor. Spare a thought for the long-suffering workers at the Ilkley Tourist Information Centre who are still having to disillusion visitors in search of this intriguing topographical feature.

As a final twist in the tale of **baht 'at**, there is its use as a registered trade mark by the Ilkley firm of Beanlands and Sons Ltd of Brook Street, grocers and provision dealers and wine and spirit merchants, established in 1869. They cashed in on the publicity provided by selling their 'Baht 'at Whisky', which was 'prepared from some of our very old bondings to a blend which is considered by experts to be far above average', and advertised along with their song-sheet. As a trade name it is still in use, by the way: they sell home-made 'Baht 'at Yorkshire Tea-bread' at White Wells.

Mutilated Versions

All kinds of strange mutations and mutilations occur in songs while they are still a matter of oral tradition. In the case of this song, the matter is further complicated by the unfamiliarity of the dialect to many of those who sing it.

A glance through collections of folk songs shows how widely varying texts can be when finally reduced to print. A good example is the song 'Widdicombe Fair', which appears in several different versions. If we take a well-known compilation of folk-songs to see how *On Ilkla Mooar* has fared, this is the kind of thing we find — in Kennedy's *Folk Songs of Britain and Ireland* (1975):

Wheear baht thee bahn when I been gone?

This is a clear misunderstanding of the dialect, as we also see in the spelling of the line:

On Ikla Moor bah t'at

The last line given in the Kennedy version shows confusion about the story as well as the dialect:

Then we shall catch t' auld cold and dee

An advert for 'Baht 'at Whisky' by Beanlands of Brook Street, Ilkley, grocers and provision dealers, attached to their issue of the song in 1927.

The trouble is that once this kind of thing gets into print it is copied and recopied, propagating versions which can become almost meaningless. Even the notes in a standard work of this kind can be misleading. The Kennedy editor states, for example, 'the author of this local dialect song is supposed to have been Thomas Clark'(!) He claims that the version he gives was sung in a more spirited way than the usual versions which are 'generally harmonised dolefully', and adds that the final lines sometimes sung are:

This is the moral of this tale: Don't go a-courtin' Mary Jane.

Spoken or shouted additions to the chorus line are another matter, and sometimes add a little zest to an authentic text. One of the earliest references to this concerns the people of Sutton, near Keighley, who traditionally shouted, after the words **baht 'at** their own addition of '**baht cap or coit**' (coat). C H Dennis records that some even changed the chorus line, after the verse about eating the ducks, so that it ran:

Wi' apple sauce, an' all!

Over the years, many choirs and other groups have added their own favourite tags, one of the more recent ones being '**Wheeare t' ducks play football**' — recent, because I think an earlier version would have said '**laik**' rather than '**play**'.

A Plea for Proper Dialect

The weirdest thing that happens to this song is the way the words are actually pronounced. It is, after all, in West Riding dialect, and deserves to be sung as near as possible with West Riding pronunciation, especially of the vowels. Just as it is only reasonable to sing *The Blaydon Races* in Geordie style, so Yorkshire people, at least, should make an effort to sing their 'anthem' as a truly Yorkshire song.

Some adjustment needs to be made, of course, by Yorkshire speakers from the North and East Ridings. I recently gave a comic dialect turn during a concert in the Swaledale Festival which I ended by getting the audience to sing *On Ilkla Mooar*. After a bit of coaching they made an excellent job of it — and most people will try to sing this in authentic style if encouraged to do so.

The main problem arises when habitual speakers of Standard English sing 'where' instead of '**whee-are**', 'were' instead of '**wor**' (actually short for 'was', not the plural), 'I' instead of '**Ah**', and — worst of all — 'On Ilkli Mawr' rather than '**On Ilkla** (or '**Ilkler**') **Mooar**'. You sometimes even hear 'bawt et' instead of '**baht 'at**'.

The West Riding way of pronouncing '**eat**' is sometimes written 'ate', which is misleading. The pronunciation is close to 'eight' ('eh-eet') and is best written **eyt**.

Notice also that the definite article, **t'** (the), is not pronounced (unless it occurs before a vowel) except as a glottal stop. So we have the line:

Then [t'] ducks 'll come an eyt up [t'] wurrums

An essential point in Yorkshire dialect in general is that some vowels are not only broad but lengthened, with a kind of double sound in words like **whee-are** and **coo-artin'**.

Of course, the northern 'u' should be used in words like '**come**' (spelling it 'coom' is misleading, as it is not a long vowel), '**ducks**' and '**up**'. To be correct the long vowel in 'Jane' should be a pure long 'e', not the dipthong 'ay-ee' or 'eye-ee' — but it is perhaps too much to expect **off-comed-uns** to attend to finer points like that!

Even worse than mutilation of the text is the distortion and mispronunciation sometimes heard even in well-meaning Yorkshire mouths. I maintain that making the effort to sing it as a true dialect song, and not as comic gibberish, only adds to the interest — and the fun.

A Unique Yorkshire Song

Whatever your opinion of *On Ilkla Mooar baht 'at*, there is no denying that it has enjoyed an immense success — and still does — carrying the name of a Yorkshire moor all round the world. But this has not always been regarded as a good thing — especially by the inhabitants of Ilkley.

Ilkley Not Amused

It is remarkable to see that in all the earlier editions of the official guides to Ilkley, there is no mention of the song that has made it a household name. By early guides I mean those in the late Victorian period, by which time we can assume the song would be well known.

The fact is that *On Ilkla Mooar* was at first an embarrassment to Ilkley. Anxious to promote its image as a genteel spa town, it must have been taken aback by the popularity of a song that might be construed as poking fun at it — a song in dialect, the uncouth speech of the cloth-capped working-class folk who came in their thousands from the industrial towns to enjoy the moor, but who contributed little to Ilkley's economy.

Reference has already been made to the graffiti carved since early Victorian times into the Cow and Calf Rocks. Abel Heywood's *Guide to Ilkley* of 1905 could not bring itself to mention the song, but it haughtily deplored the way those who must have sung it had defaced the sacred Cow:

> It exhibits the vanity and weakness of mankind in the most unmistakable manner: it is scratched and scribbled all over with names of no intent whatever to anyone but their fame-loving owners.

The belief that the residents of spa towns like Harrogate and Ilkley can be snobbish is not entirely lacking in evidence to support it. In 1936 a journalist writing in the *Yorkshire Evening Post* reported as follows:

> Ilkley people are becoming sensitive about 'On Ilkla Mooar baht 'at'. They feel that the words of the song impugn the town's reputation for decorum. 'We're a bit tired of it', an inhabitant told the *Yorkshire Evening Post*. 'There's a feeling that the song has done far more harm to the town than good'.

The writer met another resident who shared the view that the song gave the outside world absolutely the wrong impression. 'I think people get the idea that Ilkley is a bleak mill town, full of lads with mufflers and raucous voices.'

Thirty years later Bill Mitchell, then editor of *Dalesman*, still found this attitude in Ilkley. An incomer who had just moved to the West Riding told him he considered that 'the theme is downright vulgar and quite out of keeping with Ilkley's status'. When Bill Mitchell spoke to 'a friendly official' at the Ilkley Council offices, he found a more tolerant approach. It was admitted that the song tended to 'give people an impression of Ilkley as a collection of a few crofter's cottages in the middle of exposed moorland'. On the other hand, it had by this time become standard policy to print the words and music on the back of the official guide.

The policy nowadays is to make the most of the free publicity the song has provided. An official mini-guide to Ilkley, after opening with a reference to the town lying on the edge of the Yorkshire Dales National Park 'amidst some of the most spectacular and unspoilt scenery in the county', goes on to define itself as 'the town immortalised by Yorkshire's national anthem'.

Is This the Yorkshire Anthem?

In giving an account of the spoof Longfellow original from the WEA journal the *Highway*, I quoted the editor's referring to this as

'The Yorkshire Anthem'. So this was what it was being called at least as far back as the 1920s.

It is, of course, not an anthem in the sense that its first singers would have used the term — 'a solemn hymn of praise' (*OED*). There is no praise in these lyrics for anything or anybody, except perhaps the feeling that enjoyable companionship is being celebrated on Ilkley Moor. However, in the wider use of the word, 'a popular song that is identified with a person or group' (*OED*), this could surely be called an anthem. We could even go so far as to say it was an anthem in the literal sense of the word, which is derived from the Greek through Latin *antiphona*. The *OED* definition of an antiphon, 'parts ... sung or recited alternately by two groups', is exactly what the first printed version of the song was.

Although *On Ilkla Mooar* has become identified with Yorkshire, and is accepted as *the* Yorkshire song all over the county, and all over the country, it has no official status. Indeed, there are some who object to it being called the 'Yorkshire Anthem', such as the member of the Castleford male voice choir who reminded me that they always opened with 'My girl's a Yorkshire girl', which they regard as their own anthem. Annie Hinchcliffe, a keen member of the Yorkshire Society, founded in 1980 to encourage Yorkshire people to take a pride in their county, has written a 'Yorkshire Day Anthem', words and music, ending with the lines: 'Yes! We'll wear the White Rose of Yorkshire to prove our loyalty.' In 1994 my own Yorkshire Day words were published, set to the tune of *On Ilkla Mooar* for those who wanted the same music, but more modern words.

If we look for a traditional Yorkshire song to serve as the county's musical emblem, we have very little to choose from. Songs like *The Wensleydale Lad*, the story of a lad from the dale visiting Leeds, have amusing lyrics in good dialect, but they sound very dated. Then there is the delightful *Pratty Flowers*, a truly Yorkshire song:

> I will take thee to yon green gardens,
> Where the pratty, pratty flowers grow.

This became so popular in the Holme Valley area that it is still known as the 'Holmfirth Anthem' — but it is hardly ever sung in other parts of the county. Some might advocate *The Lass of Richmond Hill* as a truly representative Yorkshire song. But this, as Peter Wenham has shown, is not really of Yorkshire origin, and probably refers to the southern Richmond.

There seems to be nothing else either in Standard English or easily singable dialect, though specialist groups of folk singers have quite a repertoire of lesser-known Yorkshire songs. Of course, in this respect we are no worse off than other counties, and our Yorkshire song compares very well with such regional songs as *The Lincolnshire Poacher*, *The Derby Ram*, *Sussex by the Sea* and *I'm a Lassie from Lancashire*.

Much depends, of course, on how well and how authentically the Yorkshire song is sung. Hannah Hauxwell, with whom I recently had the pleasure of sharing a symposium on tradition and dialect, told me that she joins in the singing of *On Ilkla Mooar* on Yorkshire Day, which happens to be her birthday. She confesses it is not a special favourite of hers, but once she heard it sung by a fine baritone 'and that was a wonderful occasion'. How true it is that we so rarely do justice to this song.

Sir Bernard Ingham, whose roots are in the area from where the first singers of *On Ilkla Mooar* traditionally came, has told me that he always regarded it as 'a cautionary folk tale which reveals nature red in tooth and claw'. Then he added this delightfully forthright comment which sums up the feelings of so many of us in Yorkshire:

> What distresses me about Yorkshire's very own anthem is that it is now usually heard being murdered by people who are as incapable of appreciating the lyrics as they are of singing. Its raucous rendition has become as clichéd a picture of Yorkshire as brass bands, cloth caps, pit heaps, fish and chips, and monosyllabic morons.
>
> Yorkshire deserves better. It used to have it. I was brought up on splendid performances of the anthem by male voice choirs

who brought meaning and humour to their harmony. They took their anthem seriously. So should we.

Is This a Folk Song?

Whether or not we agree to call it 'The Yorkshire Anthem', many people would describe it as a folk song, which is how it is often listed. The question as to whether it is a folk song in the true sense of that term was raised by C H Dennis in his printed version. In his opinion it could not so be classified, 'but for two or three generations past it has had a most vigorous life, and its popularity seems as thoroughly established as that of any local folk song'.

The editor of the Beanlands edition of 1927 took Dennis up on this, suggesting that he had overstated the case. Although we have a hymn tune rather than a folk tune for the music, the words, he thought, certainly fell into the folk-song category:

> The accepted definition of 'folk song' is that it is a song or ballad originating among the people and traditionally handed down by them. To be traditionally handed down means that the song has passed from generation to generation by word of mouth, sung or spoken, and has not, for a time, been written. *Ilkla Mooar* has an oral tradition of two, if not three, generations, and, so far as that goes, it might be described as a folk song — the question can be left at that.

Even if this is not, in the strictest sense of the term, a Yorkshire folk song, what could take its place? We can compare it with songs like *Scarborough Fair*, but this is not in dialect. *Pratty Flowers*, previously mentioned, is also a real folk song, but quite localised. Then there is the oldest one of all, *The Lyke Wake Dirge* in ancient North Riding dialect, full of atmosphere, but it is, after all, a lament for the dead, with an appropriately mournful tune, and has never caught on as a popular Yorkshire song in the way that *On Ilkla Mooar* has. True, the latter also is about a burial, but it is treated with humour and sung to a triumphant tune.

A popular Bamforth cartoon postcard depicting scenes from the song — including a worm tucking in with knife and fork! (Leach Lithoprint)

I would even go so far as to say that *On Ilkla Mooar* not only has an assured place as the most popular of all Yorkshire's traditional songs, but that it is the best-known dialect song in the English-speaking world.

If we leave out Scottish and Irish songs — which are, in any case the songs of a nation, rather than a county — we have very few dialect songs from other parts to compare it with. The only dialect song to rival *On Ilkla Mooar* in popularity, in my experience, is *The Blaydon Races*, which is sung by Geordies in much the same spirit as Tykes sing their song. I would not have thought, though, that outside their respective areas, Blaydon as a place is anything like as well known as Ilkley Moor — through the songs. Still, as a truly impartial Yorkshireman I am glad to concede that *The Blaydon Races* comes a close second to *On Ilkla Mooar* in the charts.

A Universal Favourite

Here is a local song which — like the ubiquitous Yorkshire pudding — has gone round the world, especially where it has been taken by exiles from Yorkshire. Its popularity — even though many admirers do not understand it — has made it one of the landmark songs of all time, and it is significant that when the producers of a BBC Radio 4 programme were looking for interesting songs that are universally known, one of the first to occur to them was *On Ilkla Mooar*, along with other reference-point tunes such as *Happy Birthday to You* and *Amazing Grace* (another hymn tune). The writing of this book, in fact, originated when I was asked by the BBC and later ITV's *Dales Diary* to research and comment on the background to the song, something clearly of interest to people outside Yorkshire.

I would, of course, be the first to admit that Yorkshire folk do tend to push their song whenever there is an opportunity. Yet it is surprising how readily such an alien item is taken up. Many years ago I remember teaching it to a group of Scouts in Singapore — and I have heard of it being sung round camp-fires all over the world. 'Just the kind of grim, logical humour that all kids love', says Colin Speakman, recalling when he first heard it sung round a scout camp-fire in Wales. 'It came as if from nowhere. Verse after verse. And everybody knew it. I listened entranced and soon joined in'.

A colleague in the Yorkshire Dialect Society tells me that when he was with the first party of foreign tourists to enter China in 1979, because the Chinese guide asked him about his Yorkshire accent he ended up teaching the words and music of *On Ilkla Mooar* to the whole group. A former Baptist pastor has told me of a happy memory concerning a cruise to the Bahamas on the P & O liner *Oronsay*. During an informal sing-song organised for the crew and passengers in the middle of the Atlantic, he got up and to great acclaim sang all nine verses of *On Ilkla Mooar* — which previously he had also sung as a hymn.

Yorkshire servicemen have carried the song everywhere. It was, for example, the regimental song of the 2nd Battalion of the Yorkshire Volunteers. Sir Marcus Worsley (president of the Yorkshire Dialect Society) was for some years their honorary colonel, and he tells me that 'many a mess night would end up with a spirited rendering. Perhaps not everyone knew all the words but there were always enough people who did carry it through to its gruesome ending.'

When I was asking for memories connected with the song, one man phoned to say how my letter to the press had cheered him up during a period of depression, simply by bringing to mind an experience he had as a penniless student hiking through Germany with his friends. They had wandered into an inn with scarcely the price of a drink between them. Some Irish people there started singing and then asked the Yorkshire lads to sing one of their own songs. Their rendering of *On Ilkla Mooar* was rapturously received and rewarded with drinks all round. Another story I have been told was of English visitors in an Irish pub, where everybody sang in Gaelic with sly digs at the English. My friends from Yorkshire struck up in reply with *On Ilkla Mooar* — taking their revenge by singing every single verse. There is nothing new about using the song as a kind of riposte. In 1929 when Philip (Viscount) Snowden was the guest of Lloyd George, he answered a very full programme of Welsh music provided by his host by standing up and singing *On Ilkla Mooar.*

Bill Mitchell and his wife were once staying near the southern coast of Iceland. 'The air had such clarity', he writes, 'that from high ground nearby we looked across many miles of flat terrain to where snow-capped mountains stood like a tented encampment.' That evening, following their Icelandic meal, he was thinking of the Wharfedale moors 'with their dampness, mist and guttural voices of grouse' when someone suggested a sing-song. 'The first song that came to mind was *Ilkla Mooar*. Everyone, including a party of southerners, enjoyed the best known of our Yorkshire anthems.'

David Daniel, chairman of the Yorkshire Society, sums up the missionary zeal of 'baht 'at' singers in these words: 'I have sung this song in various parts of the world, including India and France.

Singers in Victorian dress at the song's centenary celebrations in 1986. (Telegraph & Argus)

Richard Whiteley with Guiseley Brass Band at the Cow and Calf Rocks, launching the Marie Curie Care Cancer Appeal. (Suzy Mortimer)

It is something which should never change. I hope it will be played and sung for ever'. Similar enthusiasm for the song is shown by the Yorkshire Ridings Society, which in 1975 started Yorkshire Day.

It is not just that travellers and exiles take the song with them to remind themselves of home, but also that foreigners sometimes learn to sing it themselves. In the 1950s a party of Russian folk-singers and dancers heard it sung by a Yorkshire coach driver while touring England. They liked it so much that their director translated it into Russian so they could sing it in their concerts and take it back home to Sverdlovsk, the most easterly city in Russia. It began in Russian (literally 'Know that I saw you') but the second line defeated the translator:

Znai je my videli tebia
On Ilkla Mooar baht 'at?

The words have been translated into other languages such as Norwegian and Danish. But some foreigners pay us the compliment of trying to master the original — like the Germans in the town of Bebra where, as mayor of Knaresborough, I had taken a town-twinning party. They gave their Yorkshire guests a surprise welcome with an excellent jazzed-up version of *On Ilkla Mooar* just to make us feel at home.

The way this song has travelled, turning up in the most unexpected places, was neatly summed up in an article by Derek Hudson in the *Yorkshire Post*, when he wrote of the tale of 'unfortunate recycling' being told 'wherever Yorkshire folk gather, when community songs are to be sung, especially beyond the boundaries of the Ridings, from Bermondsey to Bamak and Bucharest, from Reading to Reykjavik and Rotterdam, from Swansea to Sidi-bel-Abbes and San Francisco'. His article was written in 1986 to celebrate the supposed centenary of this 'sturdy, earthy anthem'.

The highlight of the centenary was a gathering of around 500 singers who wound their way up to the Cow and Calf Rocks, many in Victorian costume. The children of Addingham Middle School gave what the *Ilkley Gazette* described as 'a stirring choral and musical performance,' followed by a performance by the Cantores Olicanae and a selection of Victorian parlour songs by the operatic society — all organised by the Ilkley and Districts Arts Federation.

A similar revival of singing at the Cow and Calf Rocks took place on Yorkshire Day 1997, organised to raise money for Marie Curie Cancer Care. The fund-raising was launched the previous year by Richard Whiteley of Yorkshire Television, supported by the Guiseley Brass Band.

A Multi-purpose Melody

The strength of this song lies in its simple but memorable melody, as well as in its harmonies, and the way its four parts work so well together. As a hymn tune it has dignity and solemnity, yet with a certain vigour, even sprightliness, and an ending — again of the

Enthusiasts gathering to sing On Ilkla Mooar baht 'at *for the song's centenary celebrations held on the 21st June 1986. Eventually a total of about 500 people raised their voices in the splendid acoustics of the quarry at the Cow and Calf Rocks.* (Philip Bambridge)

utmost simplicity — which gives a feeling of confidence and triumph.

Clark's tune is so robust that you can do almost anything with it. All kinds of musical arrangements have been made of 'Cranbrook'. Paul Windrush, for example, wrote a piano piece called *Ilkley Moor*, published in 1933, which starts with a little hunting theme, followed by his own harmonisation of the *On Ilkla Mooar* tune. He also composed an 'Ilkley Moor March', and another quick-march version was adopted by the band of the Yorkshire Volunteers Regiment, formed in 1967 by the amalgamation of several Territorial Army infantry battalions. In 1991 the regimental band recorded a cassette of Yorkshire music, including this march.

Above: the author and Luke Casey during a Dales Diary *programme about the origins of* On Ilkla Mooar baht 'at.

Right: a musical jug which, when lifted, plays the tune of On Ilkla Mooar, *and is inscribed with all the verses. The jug is Crown Devon pottery dating from about 1930.*

The music is ideal for brass bands and appears, for example, as 'Theme and Variations' played by Black Dyke Mills Band and as 'The West Riding March', the signature tune of the Brighouse and Rastrick Band, who became the first-ever triple champions in 1998. This was composed for the band by Sam B Wood, who was born at Stanningley, and became the bandmaster of the 8th Battalion Leeds Rifles and was at one time the youngest bandmaster in the British Army. I am told by Ron Massey, organiser of Albert Hall concerts involving the band, that one of the great performances of *On Ilkla Mooar* was when the band accompanied a massed male-voice choir of 1,000 voices.

Alongside these full-bodied performances by choirs, including the Huddersfield Choral Society's version in its own 'Yorkshire Medley', there are all kinds of small-scale versions and variations. There was, in the 1930s, a little popular song, sold as sheet music, with ukelele parts, costing 6d, by E Leslie and J F Gilbert. Called *Sarah Jane*, it acknowledged the influence of the original in both tune and words:

> Since I caught m' death o' cold
> On Ilkla Moor baht 'at
> Where I waited in the rain,
> All these years I'm in tears —
> Where, oh where, is Sarah Jane?

This is the nearest, I think, to *On Ilkla Mooar* becoming a pop song, so perhaps we can excuse the ignorance (or poetic licence) of Mary Jane being changed to Sarah Jane. In the 1930s it was actually used as a dance tune, and recorded as such by Debroy Somers and his Band, and as a 'one-step with vocal and chorus' by Jack Jackson and his Orchestra.

As far as music for general consumption is concerned, millions of television viewers have been reminded of the tune when Yorkshire Television's logo comes up on the screen accompanied by a little musical 'ident'. This is one of many variations of 'Cranbrook' produced by the composer Chris Gunning. He demonstrated just what can be done with a tune as good as this when, in one of the special programmes for the thirtieth anniversary of YTV, he played his attractive lyrical version of it as a love song.

You never know when it is going to turn up. Bill Mitchell was once riding on one of the early diesel trains on the Bradford-Skipton line, when the driver, bored by his monotonous two-tone horn 'decided to hot-up the "doh-fah" to "doh-fah-fah-fah-doh-fah". It sounded just like the tune for *Ilkla Moor.*' Stanley Evans says that in teaching the oboe he always used the opening of the song to explain to children intervals in pitch. But nowadays, he says, it is no longer the familiar reference-point it once was, as few children learn it at school.

Over the years there have been innumerable versions as printed music and on records, tapes and discs. These range from old 78s such as a HMV record of male voice chorus and guitar (1929), and Columbia and Edison Bell records of the Sheffield Orpheus Male Voice Quartet, to all kinds of experimental versions: a vocal duet with piano, a quartet with the band of the Duke of Wellington's Regiment, Leslie Sarony, Burl Ives, flute solos, saxophone solos, mouth organ bands, and an arrangement for '12 handbells or chimes'. I have even seen a musical jug (owned by Mrs Susan Dempsey of Halifax) which plays the tune when lifted and is inscribed with all nine verses. Most interesting of all is the homage paid by a famous Lancastrian, when it was included in the 1943 Regal Zonophone record of a 'British Isles Medley' arranged for ukelele and orchestra, and sung by George Formby!

I can well understand those who say the tune gets on their nerves. Because I have been forever looking at it, and playing it, for the purpose of preparing this book, it goes on drumming away in my head, sometimes impossible to silence. But this only happens when it is misused by constant repetition. 'Cranbrook' remains a great tune — and the best compliment ever paid to it was when Eric Fenby turned it into a Rossini overture, scored for full orchestra.

Eric Fenby was the amanuensis of Delius, writing down music for the Bradford-born composer when, totally blind, he lived at

Grez-sur-Loing. The parents of Delius had rented a house on the outskirts of Ilkley, and in his youth he loved to walk over the moors. Delius and Eric Fenby must have talked about Ilkley Moor during their long collaboration, for Fenby, too, was a keen Yorkshireman, born in Scarborough. Only those who love the sparkling overtures of Rossini can appreciate the brilliance of *Rossini on Ilkla Moor* (published by Boosey and Hawkes in 1946) — an arrangement of 'Cranbrook' in the style of the Italian master, closely modelled on the classical structure of his overtures. It opens with a brisk flurry on the strings, rather like the opening of *The Silken Ladder*. Next comes a slow passage on the horns, reminiscent of *Semiramide*, for example. Then off we go, with a bubbling little tune, leading to the well-known Rossini crescendo, the music growing louder and louder, until the whole orchestra is thundering forth the music that first graced the Methodist chapels of Kent in 1805.

The Secret of Success

On Ilkla Mooar baht 'at is surely one of the hit songs of history. In modern terms it would be the envy of the pop music industry. And yet which money-spinning record company would have predicted anything good of this bizarre combination of Methodist hymn tune and dialect lyrics? So let us finally look at the reasons for the song's wide-ranging and long-lasting appeal.

First and foremost, the tune. The words ride on the back of the music, not the other way round. The examples of different arrangements we have just considered are sufficient to show that the music is both catchy and well-constructed. As an old Yorkshireman said to me recently when discussing 'Cranbrook', 'It's easy to sing — and you can give it some reight stick!'

Secondly, there is the novelty of the dialect. What was once — as we have seen — the everyday speech of West Riding working folk, now seems quaint, with the appeal of the extraordinary. As Stanley Evans points out, a phrase like **baht 'at** trips off the tongue. People enjoy singing it. Then there is the pleasurable experience of using words like **bahn**, a kind of code or strange language to some, nostalgia for others. There is also something mischievous, perhaps, about using dialect words. If you have been constrained to speak habitual Standard English with Received Pronunciation, there is a special relish in bawling out the broad vowels in **ducks** and **up**! That is, if you make the effort I have pleaded for, to sing the song in proper dialect.

Thirdly there is the humour of the sepulchral joke. As far as I can see, this is an original joke. I have not been able to find anything in the least like it in either folk tales or folk songs — though the idea of a chain of events is not unusual, as in, for example, 'For the want of a nail the shoe was lost, for the want of a shoe the horse was lost ... ' And, as we shall see, Shakespeare made a witty observation on the food chain.

Unless we can find some precedent in earlier literature or folklore, I believe we should give more credit than we usually do to the originality and ingenuity of the comic concatenation of events which are the substance of the song. It is well ahead of its time — 'the first song about recycling' as a folk singer of my acquaintance always introduces it.

The editor of the Beanlands dialogue version is one of very few to have done justice to the special attraction of the words:

> Its humour is entirely characteristic of its birthplace ... The story in the song has a delightfully West Riding stamp: a slight irregularity in behaviour ... and there is to follow illness, death, burial, a post-mortem feast for the worms, another for the domestic ducks, a third of 'funereal baked meats' ... What an appeal there is in all this, what local colour — the moorland homestead, the simple lovers, the nattering parent or friend ... One almost feels that what is chronicled in the song did really happen.

The joke is not, strictly speaking, about cannibalism, though it deliberately skates very close to it with its humorously outrageous line:

> **Then we s'll all 'ave etten thee.**

In discussing this with Dr Caroline Oates of the Folklore Society, I was interested to hear her say that almost all stories of cannibalism throughout history have been shown to be false, 'There is no evidence of any people nourishing themselves routinely with human flesh', she said, referring to the study of the subject by Walter Arens. There is such a deep-rooted taboo against cannibalism that this song, she agreed, could be seen as toying with the idea of something unthinkable. The idea holds a fascination for us, like something in a horror story. She also thought this was a Victorian moral tale — as did C H Dennis, who noted that 'all the horrors are traceable to the lad's fault'. He had, of course, behaved carelessly on the moor, and it was as though the singers were saying 'Now, look what you've made us go and do!'

A Link with Charles Darwin?

If I can make my own contribution to the discussion of where the principal idea behind the story may have come from, I suggest that it was not so much cannibalism as Darwinism. In these apparently frivolous words are overtones of the solemn theory of evolution!

It so happens that Charles Darwin, a sick man, suffering from severe stomach pains, came to stay in Ilkley in 1859, just after he had finished writing his controversial epoch-making work *The Origin of Species*. He stayed here for two months, seeking an improvement in health by taking donkey rides up to White Wells for the cold-bath treatment. He seems to have enjoyed his stay — a kind of lull before the storm — because he left Ilkley to face the uproar which followed publication.

I am not suggesting any direct connection here, but at the time the words of the song were composed, Darwin's theories would have started to percolate throughout society. Our jolly crowd of chapel-goers might not have read his book, but they could well have heard Darwin's theory of evolution denounced from the pulpit. And is it not just possible that all this talk of the survival of the fittest and the food chain — everything in nature either eating or being eaten, living on lower organisms — might have coloured their thinking?

The biological sequence man-worms-ducks-man, which most of us would rather not think about as we tuck into our meals, was brought home to the Victorians by passages in *The Origin of Species*, such as Darwin's argument that lots of cats in a certain area would mean less mice, less mice would mean more bees (on whom mice feed), and more bees would mean more clover and honey. Then there is the much-quoted closing page of his book where he invites the reader to contemplate 'worms crawling through damp earth' as part of the sequence of living things so different from eachother, yet 'dependent on eachother in so complex a manner'.

It is not surprising that Darwin mentioned worms. They were his particular favourites. He did experiments on them, wrote a treatise on them. Do I hear somebody saying, 'The song is all nonsense. Earthworms don't eat flesh!' Well, listen to Charles Darwin. Keeping his worms in pots of soil, he fed them all kinds of food to see which they preferred:

> Bits of fresh raw meat, of which worms are very fond, were fixed several times by long pins to the surface of the soil in my pots, and night after night the worms could be seen tugging at them, with the edge of the pieces engulfed in their mouths ... Raw fat seems to be preferred even to raw meat or to any other substance that was given them.

An even more grisly touch is Darwin's further observation: 'They are cannibals, for the two halves of a dead worm ... were dragged into the burrow and gnawed.' His main contention, though, was that earthworms, so disregarded and despised, have a key role in human ecology: 'Worms have played a more important part in the history of the world than most persons would first suppose'.

So we have the authority of Darwin himself, no less than the biblical text referred to earlier, to support the line:

Then t' wurrums 'll come an' eyt thee up!

Not, I repeat, a direct influence on the words of the song, but I would maintain that its neat little summary of the food chain and the interdependence of all living things, though sung in jest, could be a reflection of the Victorian preoccupation with the theory of evolution.

Before you dismiss this suggestion as too fanciful, let me tell you about a comment made by our eldest grandson, who is at a sixth form college in Stockport, taking religious studies as one of his subjects. As he is interested in dialect, I was telling him about my research into *On Ilkla Mooar*, when he astonished me by saying: 'Oh, yes. I know all about that song. Our teacher quoted it the other day ... We were discussing the difficulties in a too-literal interpretation of the doctrine of the resurrection of the body, and he used it as an illustration.'

So I submit that, although the story-line of the song seems no more than a bit of crude humour, it has a more serious side and — whether or not it reflected contemporary thinking — it can still be used to make a point in biology or theology.

A Shakespeare Original

Just before completing this book, I thought I would look through Shakespeare to see whether in this, as in so much else, he got there first. And there it was! A passage in *Hamlet* which wonderfully anticipates both Darwin and the Yorkshire song. In act 4 scene 3, the king asks Hamlet where Polonius is. Instead of saying that he is dead, Hamlet replies that he's 'at supper'. Then, with typical Shakespearean word-play on the Diet of Worms (the German city where Luther was tried before the emperor), Hamlet touches on the '**all 'ave etten thee**' topic of the song:

Hamlet: At supper ... A certain convocation of
politic worms are e'en at him. Your worm
is your only emperor for diet: we fat all
creatures else to fat us, and we fat ourselves
for maggots. Your fat king and your lean

	beggar is but variable service — two dishes, but to one table. That's the end.
King:	Alas, alas.
Hamlet:	A man may fish with the worm that hath eat of a king, and eat of the fish that hath fed of that worm.
King:	What dost thou mean by this?
Hamlet:	Nothing but to show you how a king may go a progress through the guts of a beggar.

Once again, I am not suggesting a direct influence here, but simply that the dialect words are not as daft as they seem, and have a worthy literary antecedent.

A Hardy Hybrid

If we attempt to look objectively at *On Ilkla Mooar baht 'at*, even though we may feel, as I do, that it occupies a unique little slot in the world's cultural history, we must nevertheless concede that it is only half Yorkshire.

This is hard for Yorkshire folk to take. When Wallace Harvey published his attractive sixty-four page booklet *Thomas Clark of Canterbury* in 1983, there was an outcry in Yorkshire. The front page of the *Bradford Telegraph and Argus* bore the banner headline:

We shall have to bury thee, bury thee, Mr H!

Mr Harvey was furiously pilloried for having dared to suggest 'that Yorkshire's famous anthem may have originated down south'. The lord mayor of Bradford, Mrs Joan Lightband, who happened to be an Ilkley councillor, was quoted as stating: 'It's our song. It belongs to Ilkley for all time'. She was supported by the president of Ilkley Chamber of Trade, who commented: 'It's going to take a lot to persuade people here that it's anything other than Yorkshire'.

Even national papers took up the theme, with the *Daily Mail* revealing that 'the song engraved on every Yorkshireman's heart could be a foreign import'. The report quoted Derek Broadbent, director of the Brighouse and Rastrick Band, as saying 'I'm not conceding it'. And when it was put to the landlord of the Ilkley Moor pub, Jeff Chadburn, that the tune had been written by a Canterbury cobbler, he deftly quipped 'Sounds like a load of cobblers to me!'

Of course, the general public should have known better. Wallace Harvey had launched his publication with an interview on GMTV, emphasising the importance of Clark's hymn tune. This was taken to be a new discovery, a revelation. But, in fact, the origin of 'Cranbrook' was already well known, as was pointed out by a spokesman for Bradford Cathedral and other people.

The hard historical fact is that this tune which now epitomises Yorkshire was written by a Kentish Methodist — and we should accept the fact, and be grateful to him. So hats off to Thomas Clark (and not just on the moor) whom we should make, I suggest, a posthumous honorary Yorkshireman!

The thing that has bothered some is not so much that the music is of non-Yorkshire origin as that it was for most of its life a hymn tune, with deeply religious associations. It is easy to forget nowadays just how upset many must have been when the hymn was hijacked for use as a comic song. At best it was a trivialisation, at worst sacrilege. Evidence of this was given by a woman who told *Dalesman* that her mother (born in 1882) was 'shocked and disappointed' the first time she heard 'Cranbrook' used in this way. As another correspondent commented, nowadays 'no organist dare use it'.

It is not so much that organists are reluctant to use it. 'Cranbrook' does not even appear in any current hymn book, though Clark's tune 'Crediton' is used for three hymns in the modern *Methodist Hymns and Psalms*, and as recently as 1954, when a revised edition of *The Redemption Hymnal* was published, we find that hymn 712, 'And are we yet alive?', is set to it. This is no ordinary hymn, but one written by Charles Wesley to reflect the struggles of early Methodism, when many converts suffered persecution. It is well known as the hymn always sung at the opening of the annual Methodist Conference (though nowadays to the tune 'Falcon

Street'). The last to use it were probably the Salvation Army, but since 1987 the tune has no longer appeared in their song book.

As a Methodist preacher I have occasionally revived the use of the tune for Wesley's 'O for a thousand tongues', as well as for 'While shepherd's watched'. I particularly enjoyed using the latter during a 'Tyke's Traditional Christmas' performed by the Ripon Operatic Society in 1996, as well as at 'Christmas Crack' meetings of the Yorkshire Dialect Society. This use of the tune as a Christmas carol is still found here and there in Yorkshire. Sometimes it is a family tradition, sometimes a school tradition, as it once used to be at the Christmas concerts given by Leeds Girl's High School. It is also included in the repertoire of various choirs, from the Filey Fishermen's Choir to informal Christmas concerts by York Opera, and has been sung on the Worth Valley Railway during a BBC *Songs of Praise*.

The organist and choirmaster of Bradford Cathedral, Alan Horsey, who reminds me that Ilkley Moor is slap in the middle of the Bradford Diocese, has a special fondness for 'Cranbrook', which he always uses with the cathedral choir at Christmas, including at the Grassington Dickens Festival. 'It gives an emotional lift to "While Shepherds watched"', he says. 'It's a real winner.'

'Cranbrook' is a splendid tune for 'While shepherds watched', especially when you sing three exultant times 'And glory shone around!'. It is not always easy to make an adjustment, however. His Grace the Archbishop of York has told me of his own experience when 'some of our more adventurous directors of music are known, on occasion to discard the tried and trusted "Winchester Old" in favour of "Cranbrook"':

> At most of the church services which I attend these days (and carol services are no exception), I find myself placed in full view of the whole congregation — so that the ability to keep a straight face is a must! However, I have to confess that, inside the archi-episcopal persona, there lurks that 'other me' — the one who, when he hears a band or organ strike up with 'Cranbrook', is conjuring with the deliciously illicit thought that this just might

be the time when someone is going to do the unthinkable — and launch himself wholeheartedly into Yorkshire's national anthem!

Still, this problem caused by the secularisation of a religious song is only for an older generation. Young people nowadays rarely sing hymns, or formal songs of any kind, especially in dialect. Just before starting on this final chapter, I took some of my grandchildren on the classic walk from Dick Hudson's over the moor. Up on the top, surrounded by heather in bloom, I tried to teach them to sing *On Ilkla Mooar baht 'at.* They had all been brought up in Yorkshire, but it was like teaching them a foreign language, and reminded me of my days in the classroom, when I used to teach French, including French folk-songs.

Yet I think it is worth making the effort to keep a piece of our heritage alive. What a curious phenomenon this is! A bit of good-natured teasing in homely dialect, a celebration of love, a mock-lament for the dead and the ironies of human existence ... Something so slight and ephemeral — yet, married to this melody, it lives happily ever after.

The story of its origin is still a matter of romantic legend rather than historical fact. The authors of the dialect lyrics remain anonymous, just like the lad who courted Mary Jane. And if they had chosen almost any other hymn tune, their words would probably have been lost for ever, and we would have been deprived of this strange, distinctive hybrid, a song like no other in the world.

As it is, we have something here that adds a dab of local colour to the blanket of monotonous grey uniformity that threatens to spread over modern life. And as a Methodist, I like to think that it was chapel-goers with a sense of humour who unknowingly made a contribution to Yorkshire's rich heritage. I regret that, as a consequence, one of our best hymn tunes is no longer generally sung as such. But the Church's loss is surely Yorkshire's gain.

Chronological Summary

1775	Birth of Thomas Clark of Canterbury, Methodist cordwainer and choirmaster
1788	Death of Charles Wesley, Methodist hymn-writer
1791	Death of John Wesley, leader of the Methodist Revival
1805	Publication of 'Cranbrook', typical early Methodist hymn tune
1811	Opening of St Peter's Methodist Chapel, Canterbury
1837	Publication of Clark's influential *Union Tune Book*. 'Cranbrook' becomes increasingly popular as a hymn tune, especially in Yorkshire, where in the second half of the century words in West Riding dialect are sung to it. Tradition suggests origin during or shortly after an outing to Ilkley Moor by a chapel choir, probably Methodist, probably from the Halifax area. This supported by the question-and-answer style of the earliest published version. Less likely that it originated at an indoor evening gathering or was written by an individual.
1856(?)	Earliest date for dialect version (Dennis estimate)
1867(?)	Later suggested date (Beanlands estimate)
1877(?)	Sung by the Heptonstall Glee Choir (Wallace Harvey)
1886(?)	Traditional date for Halifax choir outing to Ilkley Moor
1897	Public performances of song (eg in Scarborough)
1916	First published version (C H Dennis, Huddersfield)
1927	Second published version (Beanlands & Sons, Ilkley)
1929	First commercial recordings of the song
1944	*West Riding March* by Sam B Wood (Brighouse and Rastrick Band)
1946	*Rossini on Ilkla Moor*, overture by Eric Fenby
1986	Centenary celebrations, Cow and Calf Rocks
1997	Yorkshire Day sing for Marie Cure Cancer Care
1998	Featured on ITV's *Dales Diary*

This version of the music is based on the one given by C H Dennis. He changed the key from two sharps into natural, and unfortunately mis-copied or altered the first **baht** *in the refrain so that it dropped only to B instead of G — losing Clark's original interval of a 4th, which I have restored in this easy-to-sing version.* *For the words see page 75.*

Bibliography

A Thousand Miles in Wharfedale (1892), Edmund Bogg.
Upper Wharfedale (1900), Harry Speight.
The Haunted Moor (1934), Nicholas Size.
Rombalds Way: A Pre-history of Mid-Wharfedale (1946), E T Cowling.
Spas of England I (1841), A B Granville.
Ilkley: The Victorian Era (1986), David Carpenter.
Yorkshire Walks from Bradford (1938), 'Wanderer' (Eric Lodge).
Ilkley Moor Souvenir and Guide (1985), West Riding Ramblers' Association.
The Journal of John Wesley (8 vols) (1938), ed Nehemiah Curnock.
Hymns for the People called Methodists (1780), ed John Wesley.
The Methodist Hymn Book (1933).
The Music of the Methodist Hymn Book (1935), J T Lightwood.
After Wesley (1935), Maldwyn Edwards.
The Romance of Our Old Village Choirs (1942), R C Morrell.
Thomas Clark of Canterbury (1983), Wallace Harvey.
A Set of Psalms and Hymn Tunes (1805), Thomas Clark.
The Union Tune Book (1837), ed Thomas Clark.
Basic Broad Yorkshire (1992), Arnold Kellett.
The Yorkshire Dictionary of Dialect, Tradition and Folklore (1994), Arnold Kellett.
Yorkshire Lyrics (1898), John Hartley.
Reminiscences of a Bradford Mill Girl (1980), Maggie Newberry.
Maps & Views of Old Halifax (1991), ed A Bettridge, D Bridge.
The White Rose Garland (1949), ed W J Halliday and A S Umpleby.
Ranters, Revivalists, etc (1996), D Colin Dews.

On Ilkla Moor baht 'at (1916), ed C H Dennis.
On Ilkla Moor baht 'at (1927), ed for Beanlands & Sons.
The 42nd (East Lancs) Division, 1914-1918 (1920), F P Gibbon.
Folk Songs of Britain and Ireland (1975), ed Peter Kennedy.
The Lass of Richmond Hill (1986), Peter Wenham.
Music of the Yorkshire Dales (1997), W R Mitchell.
The Man-Eating Myth (1979), Walter Arens.
The Origin of Species (1859), Charles Darwin.
The Formation of Vegetable Mould through Action of Worms (1881), Charles Darwin.
The Arden Shakespeare: Hamlet (1982), ed Harold Jenkins.

Many other books have been consulted, and especially journals and newspapers. These include, in addition to various Yorkshire almanacks and Ilkley guidebooks, the *Highway*, *Dalesman*, *Yorkshire Life*, *Yorkshire Post*, *Yorkshire Evening Post*, *Bradford Telegraph & Argus*, *Keighley News*, *Ilkley Gazette*, etc.

There are about fifty different vocal and instrumental recordings of the song, most of these being held in the National Sound Archive.